Creating a Green and Cultural Economy:

A story from India that integrates the best in East & West

Ram Ramprasad

iUniverse, Inc.
Bloomington

Creating a Green and Cultural Economy
A story from India that integrates the best in East & West

iUniverse books may be ordered through booksellers or by contacting:

iUniverse
1663 Liberty Drive
Bloomington, IN 47403
www.iuniverse.com
1-800-Authors (1-800-288-4677)

Because of the dynamic nature of the Internet, any web addresses or links contained in this book may have changed since publication and may no longer be valid. The views expressed in this work are solely those of the author and do not necessarily reflect the views of the publisher, and the publisher hereby disclaims any responsibility for them.

Any people depicted in stock imagery provided by Thinkstock are models, and such images are being used for illustrative purposes only.

Certain stock imagery © Thinkstock.

ISBN: 978-1-4620-1602-0 (sc)
ISBN: 978-1-4620-1603-7 (ebook)

Library of Congress Control Number: 2011906668

Printed in the United States of America

iUniverse rev. date: 5/16/2011

In memory of my beloved father

Dr. L.Venkataratnam

(March 1, 1919 – July 2, 2002)

One of India's most eminent horticulturist

The world is too much with us; late and soon,
Getting and spending, we lay waste our powers;
Little we see in Nature that is ours;
We have given our hearts away, a sordid boon!
--William Wordsworth

Contents

Acknowledgements   ix

Introduction   xi

1   The Richness of Biodiversity   **1**
To My Motherland   2
The Song of Trees   5
Trees Survived Killari Earthquake in Maharashtra   6

2   Sustainable Living in the 1960s   **8**
Sustainable Living in the 60s   8

**3   A Comparison Between Pre-mid 1960s
     and Post- mid 1960s**   **13**
Fostering Diversity   13
Life in the Developing World   15
The Story of Zindabad -- A Lesson in Sustainable Living
(Part 1 of 4)   17
Moral of Part 1 of the Story   20

4   Ecology and Human Health   **22**
Ecology and Human Health   23

5   The Population Dilemma   **25**
The Population Dilemma   26

6   Definition of Growth   **29**
Current Definition Of Growth   29

7   The Dilemma of Economics   **34**
The Story of Zindabad (Part 2 of 4)   34
The Dilemma of Economics   37

8   Education Methods — The Crux of the Problem   **40**
Education – Reflections on an Approach   40

9   A Simple Guide to Sustainable Living   **45**
A Simple Guide to Attaining Sustainable Living   45
The Story of Zindabad (Part 3 of 4)   48
Conclusion of the Story   59
East and West — Achieving Perfection by
Understanding Imperfection   60
Capitalism Versus Communism   64

10 Buckling up to Restore Our Ecosystem   **67**
Buckling Up   68
The Story of Zindabad (Part 4 of 4)   69
Sixty–Five Years of Environmental Independence   86

11 Establishing a Framework for Creating a
Cultural Economy   **89**

Afterword   **105**
First Steps to Building a Cultural Economy   107

Footnotes   **113**

References   **117**

Acknowledgements

I thank the following institutions and individuals:

- My father, Dr. L. Venkataratnam, and my mother, Mrs. Sarojiniratnam, for being the source and inspiration for this book.
- All individuals and institutions engaged in the healing process of the earth and its magnificent beings, where writings and actions inspire confidence that there is hope.
- Cathy R. Dickinson and Anita Gogno for editing the final manuscript with keen enthusiasm.
- My wife, Gayathri, and my two sons, Varun and Vinay, for their support.
- My friend Ratan Dadichi for his encouragement

Introduction

Most of us have at some time or other sat down and wondered about how our working lives should be. At times, we feel so occupied with hectic work schedules and family activities that we just move on mechanically with our lives. We feel something was taken from us, and yet we are not so sure what it is. We all know we have to make money; we get so engrossed in the rat race that we do not seem fully satisfied. Cost of living keeps rising, and financing an education (in all parts of the world) costs a small fortune. Without two people working, we feel there is no way one can make ends meet. We worry about our children's education, our health care, and old age.

At the same time, we want to have some relief from life's everyday chores and to have some fun as well. We read all kinds of magazines, listen to news on the television, stay connected with the Internet, and make sure we are constantly aware of what is going on in this world. But sometimes we still feel empty. We want to articulate our thoughts in public, and social media make it easier than ever to do so. But it is risky to talk about things like ecology, our spiritual selves, or other issues so personal to our lives. Environmental problems are an everyday occurrence that we have come to accept. When did we stop asking, "how can we as individuals make any difference?" I believe the answer lies in these personal aspects that, when related to our social, cultural, and physical environments, can have the most impact on our lives.

We often ignore the obvious economic and environmental problems that afflict society and, instead, through the manipulative aspects of science, economics, politics, and sociology we are fixated on solutions. We create products, systems, and services that emphasize fixing individual parts of the system, ignoring their impact on the whole system. We pursue the more obscure phenomena of matter and nature because we tend to believe that an emphasis on reductionism and top-down solutions will cure society's problems.

We all know that the whole is greater than the sum of its parts, but we continue to manipulate the parts and thus adversely impact the whole. A holistic understanding of the whole and the interrelationship it has with its parts may need more attention for creating a well-balanced economy. A well-balanced economy needs to address the triad of sustainable development, ie, economy, equality, and ecology, in a holistic manner.

What I discuss in the book is obvious: A focus on the whole. Finding solutions to the obvious can make the most meaningful impact on our lives. This approach can be more significant than dwelling solely on the obscure or the individual parts that impact any system. There is merit in placing emphasis on both the whole and the parts. However, in focusing on the parts without looking at the whole, we distort the emphasis, intention, and results of our endeavors.

I am simply talking ecological issues and sustainable living within the framework of ecological issues. These are the obvious issues in any society, and ecosystems, by their very definition, embrace all parts of the earthly household. I choose to convey this message through poetry interlaced with storytelling. I also embellish storytelling with nonfiction examples and facts to entertain you in matters such as ecology, environment, and economics. I hope after reading this book you will walk away with the feeling that you learned something; perhaps with some thoughts on becoming a nature entrepreneur or an eco-entrepreneur.

I'm not sure why I ventured to write this book. Maybe it was one of those creative endeavors where I wanted to capture and share my thoughts and feelings on our state of affairs. In my own way, I wanted to take stock of what I had done for the world or the country that gave birth to me. So, in a simple poetic story I decided to share this feeling. I attribute any insights in my poetry to the wonderful force that feeds our minds and nourishes our thoughts. We sometimes wonder whether this force is generated within us or outside of us, or if it simply develops from the knowledge we gather over time. Perhaps it is a combination of all these. Anything that people consider offensive, I attribute to my own foibles that may have tainted my thinking. We all lead the lives with an amalgam of thoughts that are good, bad, and simply ignorant.

We are always constantly battling within ourselves to balance our thoughts with appropriate actions. We desire our thoughts to produce actions that are meaningful to both society and nature. But how much are we trained to undertake such tasks? Even in this book, I sometimes struggled to accomplish the same. It is a delicate act to write book that is both good for the society and nature. But this is the true challenge for all individuals – to do not just what is good for society but also to do what is good for the whole and for nature. I made an attempt to balance constructive criticism with hope and not despair. I tried to reflect my own mental struggles with life, perhaps in an attempt to draw the reader in a collective pursuit where we all can face the vicissitudes of life in a simple manner. I made a simple attempt at this. None of us will ever be able to change our world overnight. But we certainly can make a slow and a steady progress in our everyday actions. Our actions will determine our quality of our lives for our children and the future generations. This is what the book is about – living in a sustainable manner within the context of our culture. When people live in a sustainable manner, they transform economics within the context of any culture. For example, a consumer economy could be transformed to a cultural economy. I address several benefits of such a transformation in this book. While the book is written in the context of the Indian economy, most of the concepts may have a universal appeal and applicability in the West as well as the East.

I don't know why I chose a hybrid of poetry, storytelling, and non-fiction prose to convey these feelings. I may have chosen poetry because I could not say it in any better manner. Diane Ackerman, a poet, essayist, and a naturalist, in her book, *Deep Play,* describes poetry in this way: "A poem is where an emotional or metaphysical truce takes place. A poem knows about illusion and magic, how to glorify what is not glorious, how to bankrupt what is. It displays, in its alchemy of mind, the transmuting of the commonplace into golden saliences. A poem records emotions and moods that lie beyond normal language that can only be patched together and hinted at metaphorically. It knows about spunk, zealousness, obstinacy, and deliverance."[1]

Therefore, I chose poetry to glorify the things that seem to have become meaningless in society, issues such as our environment and ecology. Poetry was used to theorize the subject matter of cultural economy and sustainable living, while storytelling was used to embellish the meaning that was created in the poems.

Storytelling, in four parts, is spread across four different chapters. The setting of the story is in a fictional city called Zindabad in India. The plot is interlaced with nonfiction messages to convey a reflection on our state of affairs. The art of sustainable living is created in this story to demonstrate the benefits of living and creating a cultural economy. The momentum and the drama of the story capture real-life situations in a fictional format. The action takes place in the midst of bustling city life. This is the thesis of the book – to convey a personal opinion and offer the solution of a people-initiated economic plan (as opposed to a government-initiated economic plan) for India conveyed through poetry and storytelling.

Ram Ramprasad

1

The Richness of Biodiversity

I left India at the age of twenty-two for a teaching position in Africa. After teaching there in a University for a little over five years, I left for America for a graduate degree program and I continue to live here. However, I do visit my parents once every few years. But sometimes the demands of the job or squeezing vacation time occasionally stretches things beyond what one in India would consider often enough. However, my loving parents never complained about the timeliness, or the untimeliness, of our visits, They have always just felt happy to see my family.

At the age of ten, I developed asthma in India, sometime in the mid-1960s. Instinctively, I knew this had nothing to do with the genetic inheritance, although local doctors would simply attribute this to genetic phenomena (that I must have inherited from an uncle or a grandparent). Hyderabad, where I lived, was slowly getting polluted. When it rained in Hyderabad the Hussain Sagar Lake emitted an odor that triggered an asthmatic reaction in my body. This was an observation of my body's rhythms, that I attributed to pollution of the lake with industrial effluents. After I left Hyderabad for Africa, my asthma disappeared and never returned. But memories of my asthma, triggered by pollution, remain.

From the ages of four through twenty-two, I remember my early years both in New Delhi and in Hyderabad. The early years were marked with a sense of awe for everything that I saw in India and the life I spent at my house in Hyderabad. One cannot imagine the natural wonder that existed in the early 1950s and 1960s in New Delhi and Hyderabad. It now seems to have disappeared. What follows is a story of the land that gave birth to me: a pre- and a post comparison using mid 1960s as the benchmark for comparison.

The day I left India, my friend, Ratan, gave me a poem he had written. To this day he continues to be a true lover of his country and a cultural spiritualist. His poem celebrates the majesty of India. I consider it a hymn, and thought it would be appropriate for the opening chapter of this book. I was amazed at the wonder Ratan saw at such an early age in the land he loves so much. As adults, we sometimes do not know the potential we had as young children. Reading this poem perhaps gave me insight to recapture that youth I really was. When I shared it with him later, Ratan was quite surprised that he could have written such a poem at such an early age. He did not even recall writing it until I showed him his own handwritten words.

To My Motherland

by Ratan Dadhichi, Hyderabad, India (1976)

Hail to Thee, my ancient and glorious Motherland,

Hail O Mother, with Thy rivers eternal and fertile land.

Crowned with Himalayan peaks of Shiva's snowy abode,

With Thy feet resting gracefully on Rama's ancient road.

Thy gentle arms reach the oceans East and West,

And holy rivers flow from Thy motherly breast.

Thy fruits and corn smile with golden zest,

And make, O Motherland, a paradise thrice blest.

Thy mountains are nurseries for the Spirit's communion,

Where sages and saints meet in holy union.

Thy sons, O Mother, speak in many a tongue,

And yet Thy beauties have never remained unsung.

Brahma, Vishnu, and Mahesh, Thy altars adorn,

Rama, Krishna and Buddha were in Thy cradle born.

Thou Mother of Saints and Gods, how eternal Thou art,

O Motherland, Thou art the smile and sigh of my heart.

Where is the land as hallowed as Thee, O Motherland,

The cradle of a human race as ancient as Thy soil and sand.

Call me again and again to Thy breast, O Mother Divine,

Pray, send me not to another lap to languish and pine.

Hail to Thee, my ancient and glorious Motherland,

Hail O Mother, with Thy rivers eternal and fertile land.

For some odd reason, I filed Ratan's poem along with all of my important degree certificates. About 10 years ago, I stumbled on the poem and, for some reason, it hit home.

Strangely enough, I visited India the same year I found the poem. During that visit I was not sure that we were making any wholesome progress at all. I have intentionally chosen the word: "wholesome" because the word "holy" is derived from the word "whole."

The local newspapers for overseas Indians always touted our economic progress and the export of software to America and Europe. People in India were proud that they matched American standards. Family and friends would boast that India could now supply any Western product in its stores. My family and I, having become accustomed to several Western tastes, were quite happy to feel at home. Cereals, fruit juices, tissue rolls, shaving blades, decaffeinated coffee, you name it, and you had it. My family and friends were delighted that we could have it all. The generosity of my family and friends was unbelievable.

Yet at the same time, I sensed my father's unhappiness. His work revolved around horticulture. An agriculturist by training, he was always candid with his children that he had two wives: one my mother, and the other his profession as a horticulturist. He was troubled at what was happening with the country. He related a story to me that he wanted to start a curbside trash collection and recycling program in the colony, but most people were not ready to pay a reasonable monthly fee. On the contrary, most were happy dumping trash just a few houses away from ours on an open land. The sight of the garbage mountain right in the midst of a well-developed neighborhood was very unsettling. A true volunteer at heart, this troubled his psyche. He somehow managed to pull through a Hyderabad Bachao Program (Save Hyderabad). Finally, through the cooperation and leadership of several of his friends, he managed to convince the right authorities to clean up the garbage mountain and the Hussain Sagar Lake in Hyderabad.

He was not only a social worker but also an author of agriculture-related articles and books. He wrote the poem below at a ripe age of 82. I accidentally saw it on his desk during my visit. He was a little embarrassed when I read his poem. But I was so proud that he had attempted to write and publish it. I am still not certain whether the poem was published in the local newspaper as he had planned. On that visit, I "stole" a copy of his poem and then sought his permission to keep it. My father's poem shows the pain he felt at the destruction of the trees in India. I share with you the poem, along with the letter he wrote to the local newspaper seeking its publication.

The Song of Trees

by Dr. L. Venkataratnam, Chairman

Agri-Horticultural Society, Hyderabad

(Written sometime in 2000)

The sacred earth is our mother,

The bright sun is our father.

We are not mobile as you are,

We will not survive if you dare,

We grow with your care,

Birds nest in our branches.

They help us to multiply in ranches,

We can survive if they cut us.

But you cannot survive without us,

Our journey is till eternity.

For we have to serve the posterity,

You cut our limbs for all festivities.

We never frown on these activities,

We live in villages and cities.

But people in cities do not care,

Yet, we try to grow everywhere.

We are destined by men to be cut,

But we still yield fruits for them to eat.

We can still survive if they hate us,

But they cannot survive without us.

Trees Survived Killari Earthquake in Maharashtra

(My father's letter to the local newspaper
that accompanied the poem)

"Last year the day after the Ganesh Chathurthi festival, the earthquake destroyed thousands of houses, cattle, men and its devastating effect caused a losses of over Rs10,000 crore. This forecast is well known to our country. But one good feature that escaped the attention of the public at large is the survival of the trees. In this region, *Ramkat, Babul, Neem, Tamarind, Karanj, Ficus* are the common trees. Not a single tree was uprooted. These trees had a firm foothold on mother earth. This natural affinity of the trees with Mother Earth protects them. It is this <u>reciprocal</u> love with Mother Earth that the earthquake did not disturb them.

"Roads are being laid, houses are being built, electricity is being restored, schools are being rebuilt, hospitals are being restored, but the trees are being forgotten in the program for rehabilitation. Let every house have a few trees, and let the victims of the earthquake love and protect these trees. In the sun, they will protect them when the earthquake destroys everything else. Then I ask, why is the public so partial that they cannot undertake serious tree planting with economic trees that will maintain our ecosystem?"

What struck me with the letter and the poem was his deep understanding of the word "reciprocal" that I have underlined. He once commented to me that a possible cause of the earthquake was oil drilling. He provided me with an analogy: consider what would happen if we take the cartilage fluid out of a human being's knee—the bones in the person's knee would rub against each other and cause severe pain. Similarly, my father said the same could be said about the tectonic plates of the earth: removing the joint fluid of the earth (oil) may cause problems such as an earthquake. I present his opinion as a hypothesis that may need further research by geophysicists and geologists.

Every environmentalist and ecologist seems to have an innate understanding of the law of "reciprocity." My father is certainly not the kind of person who would visit a temple frequently. His temple was the tree, the garden, the land, and nature.

E.O. Wilson, the famous Harvard biologist coined the term 'biodiversity." This word became a household word for my father. Another term coined by a naturalist that described him well is "ecospirituality." I truly think my father, in his heart, was an ecospiritualist and a specialist in biodiversity. Sometimes I come across others who were like him or I hear about them and their in the news. Then there are so many others like him who go could care less whether the world notices their work or not. All of these people are the true karma yogis of our land.

2

Sustainable Living in the 1960s

Let's now go back in time and trace the pre-mid 60's life that I enjoyed with my family. After reading the poem below, we need to question ourselves on the meaning of the word "progress" in India. The important question to assess from the poem is the meaning of true sustenance. The intention of the poem is not to draw the reader into any kind of story on my personal family life, but to reflect on our lives on how it was in the 1960s (at least for those of us who have already reached their mid-50s or older.)

Sustainable Living in the 60s

My Mom, the beautiful,

My Dad, the strong,

Together they supported the six of us.

True souls living in perfect communion with nature,

The house we lived was a haven for recycling,

Orange peels were made into pickles,

Seeds of mango, papaya, and grape were given to the farmers,

Plastic bags were knitted into delightful mats.

The leftover milk was converted to curried dish,

The fresh mud of earth was used to clean pots and pans,

The humble cow with an abode in our backyard gave us milk

Its sprayed dung kept the insects away from our house.

We shampooed with Shika nuts,

My sister rejuvenated her face with turmeric,

Not one tooth lost at 84, my father brushed with his finger, and tooth powder.

My mother knew all the old grandma remedies,

Yet, when the time was right

She rushed my brother to the hospital for an appendectomy.

They faced vicissitudes with common sense,

But, surprisingly, they communed with nature,

I was bitter as the youngest wearing recycled clothes,

But, alas, I knew their wisdom,

I read comics and magazines from the circulating vendor library,

Newspapers were sold back to the recycling vendor.

My father taught the neighbors kitchen gardening skills,

He appeared on radio and TV teaching bonsai.

In his spare time, if he ever had,

He invented, through natural means, a custard-apple without seeds.

He was honored with an Honorary Doctoral degree from America.

I read all about it in my Telugu language textbook in my 6th grade class.

Back then,

Doctoral degrees were awarded when people developed simple

Solutions to complex problems.

Now,

Doctoral degrees are awarded when people develop complex

Solutions to simple problems.

My mother reveled in her culinary skills,

She bagged prizes in national contests,

She had an art of transforming even grated potato skin to a culinary dish,

Nothing was wasted in her presence,

She watered our kitchen garden with water from the well,

And bartered plantains and sapota fruit for guava and papaya

She nourished our supple bodies with a wide variety of fruit,

Cross –legged we ate breakfast, lunch, or dinner,

Instinctively, she knew this would help prevent an arthritic joint.

She celebrated every festival with zest and zeal,

Stringing garlands of flowers with jasmine and hibiscus,

She woke us up at 4 am on the nights of Divali,

And made us crack the early morning dawn with incense and firecracker.

Dad and Mom created magic in our house,

Everything was recycled and nothing was polluted,

Not the water that left our drains,

Nor the air that breezed through our windows

Although I was only a child in the pre-mid 1960s, I realized that India was a cultural economy. People understood ecology within the context of a deep and rich culture. The entire fabric of the community was designed in such a way that the day-to-day habits of the people, their way of life, the business economy, the technological structures, and the physical structures did not interfere with nature's inherent ability to sustain life. For example, even the kitchen utensils in my house were not cleaned with a sponge (created with a petrochemical base); they were cleaned with coconut husks. I hope some can relate to the examples cited in the poem above with a sense of nostalgia. I simply reflect and think about the pre-mid 1960s wisdom where nothing that left our house was polluted. The water that left our drains only had organic or biological waste. There was no trace of detergent, soap, toxic chemical, or even toilet tissue paper. Did our culture somehow know not to mix industrial sludge with biological sludge? Maybe our culture also knew that such activities would only produce toxic fertilizer that through plants would find their way back into our bodies. Introspectively, I marveled at the culture that so deeply influenced a sustainable and an ecological culture. How did this happen? What was the basis?

Now, let us also see how India was historically so that we can get a better understanding of why India was a cultural economy and whether this kind of cultural economy supported an ecologically appropriate lifestyle. About 200 years ago, India was ruled by kings who were dishonest and corrupt, but the water management tradition of India was healthy. There were hundreds of thousands of tanks all over India, on which the villagers and townspeople depended to survive. The kings never made these tanks; it all happened because of a decentralized form of government in which the communities had control of natural resources. People made channels to bring water to the tank, and they would make sure that no one could pollute the channel or the watershed. According to Anil Agarwal, an environmentalist who passed away, "Today nobody cares—not the government or the citizens." I wonder whether this is because we have become alienated from the rich aspects of our culture.

There are some key takeaways from this chapter:

- the focus on natural resources must fall back into the hands of the community.
- both the people and the government need to become more sensitive to balancing development with ecology.
- a revival of an almost forgotten ecologically oriented culture needs to be reestablished.
-

These criteria are the underlying theme of the succeeding chapters, with several clues on how to accomplish these objectives through a slow and methodical approach.

3

A Comparison Between Pre-mid 1960s and Post- mid 1960s

The pre-mid 60s, in my opinion, were marked with great diversity in India; I am not certain how many of the elements of this diversity we retain. This is one of those nostalgic poems that shows the strength of diversity I remember.

Fostering Diversity

The all-beautiful Mother Nature,

So rich and so glorious in your diversity,

You show strength in your diversity,

But become weak bereft of it.

The multicolored plants, leaves, and flowers you carry,

The buzzing multitude of insect species you hold,

Multicolored humanity revel and rejoice in your strength,

Delighting the air with a sweet diversity of language and dialect.

Thou, so endowed with luscious fruits and vegetables,

The pure water streams cleanse your body,

The bright morning sunshine bathes you so clean,

The crackling wind cheers and freshens your ever delightful self.

The puffy tufts of clouds add thy beauty to your winsome face,

The chirping birds sing and delight in your melodious glory,

Blue whales and dolphins come out of their abode and envy your charm,

The sun and the moon, your guardian angels, love you like their own.

Whatever happened to all that diversity you hold,

Oh Mother Nature, your strength is diversity,

Not the displacement of it,

Oh Mother Nature, give us the wisdom to live and not disrupt your diversity.

On my visits to India, I constantly felt we had lost touch with nature. I felt my friends and family could not even talk about what they had lost. After all, we are not going to complain to our physicians and friends that nature indeed was providing us with a therapeutic value that we somehow suddenly felt were missing in our lives. The post 60s phenomenon was marked by a rapid deterioration in our environment. The population had more than tripled since the time I left India. The number of cars spewing their leaded gasoline emissions choked the roads of Hyderabad. Ironically, the government was subsidizing diesel that was more harmful than even the leaded gasoline.

My neighbor complained and lived in constant fear that her house would one day fall prey to the gigantic highways that the Andhra Pradesh government was planning to build. I questioned why the flyover was needed. Why was prime land destroyed for building roads and urbanization? Why were trees uprooted for the sake of flyovers? While most knew something wrong was happening, they felt reluctant to admit this in public. They thought they would be ridiculed. A dominant section of the people felt the solution for traffic was to build more roads, flyovers, and highways.

I wondered whether these people read the book *State of the World* published by the World Watch Institute in Washington, D.C. USA. The workers at this institute such as Lester Brown and Christopher Flavin did some sincere and genuine work in sustainable development. Nevertheless, I was not ready to argue with anyone. I would have been asked to mind my own business since I didn't live in India anymore. But my parents, my brother, relatives and friends still live in Hyderabad. However, the care was genuine and extended for the population as a whole. The poem below shows my post-60s feelings.

Life in the Developing World

The motorcar squeaks,

... and the oil leaks,

The leaded fumes escape the broken tailpipe,

The early morning haze so filled with smoke.

The teeming population gives their lackadaisical yawn,

Getting ready to break the dawn,

The will to energize almost seems so lost,

While pulling themselves up at every cost.

They roll up their sleeves and get ready for work,

In traffic jams, they toil and honk,

Perspiring in the hot sun and polluted air,

They wonder if the world has some care.

Struggle they do to live a life,

It is almost certain it is not without a strife,

Enslaved in environmental degradation,

They seek solutions for the next generation.

With hope and courage, they set to fight dilapidation,

But mesmerized they become in the charm of globalization,

In utter consternation, reason rules over instinct,

The dominance of growth over nature again becomes distinct.

Let's talk here a little bit more about diversity. While the dictionary meaning of diversity is restricted to a sense of variety, we may have limited ourselves with the mechanical aspect of this definition. Diversity, I think, means much more. An expanded definition of diversity is not just the nature of variety, but the ability to hold, assimilate, and cherish this variety with harmony and balance that seems to have the most beneficial effect for the entity or the organism in question.

As children we were used to being told stories to convey the full potential of a word, a theme, a moral, or something where complex amounts of information could be absorbed in an easy and imaginative manner. While I tried to look for a story on diversity, I just couldn't find one. So, similar to telling an imaginary bedtime story for my children when they were young, I simply made up a story to convey the meaning of the word "diversity" that is inextricably linked with wholesome living.

The Story of Zindabad -- A Lesson in Sustainable Living (Part 1 of 4)

In a bustling city called Zindabad there once lived a farmer, his wife, and two children. The farmer owned a nursery business that grew several varieties of rose plants. His nursery was very popular and was frequently visited by the folks in the town. They loved this family so much that they gave the family a nickname, Mr. & Mrs. Gulab Raja (the Rose King and the Rose Queen). Their son was nicknamed Gulab Raja Jr. and the daughter Gulab Rani.

Gulab Raja used to sell both cut roses and full rose plants. Mrs. Gulab Raja used to manage all the finances and was an exceptional salesperson. While she, like her farmer husband, had no formal education, she was considered a woman with a lot of common sense. She used to read wonderful tales from the epics to her children when they were young. The people in the town thought that she was not only a good salesperson but also someone who gave them a lot of wisdom on how to grow rose plants. The farmer was considered a very hardworking man who always kept the nursery in full bloom and attended to all the chores of the business. The farmer's grown-up daughter was a major in sociology, and the son was considered an ambitious young plant biologist of high repute. Both children helped their parents in the business. The son built, for his father, a small greenhouse to take care of the young tender plants so that they would not die of the scorching summer heat of the tropics. The daughter used to teach the mother and the father how to work with the customers. Her advice on customer service vastly improved the business. Things for the most part were going well.

One day the son started experimenting with the rose plants. He, through several scientific means, could now produce red rose plants of a different variety. The following are the different categories of rose plants the farmer now produced:

a) The natural plant had 30 leaves for every one rose.

b) The experimental plant had 10 roses for every one leaf.

Some had six roses to one leaf and so on, In general he had more roses on a plant than leaves.

The daughter, being a major in sociology, convinced her parents that a good market research survey of the customers would determine consumer preference and attitudes for various red rose plants. The results of the survey revealed the following:

a) The consumers generally seemed to like the natural rose plant because of the following reasons:

-The roses and the leaves seemed to be in perfect balance. The balance added perfect beauty.

-The roses on the natural plants seemed to have a different shape, size, texture, and richness of color.

Therefore, people seemed to enjoy them more when they planted these in their gardens.

-However; a segment of the population did not seem to care about the shape, size, and texture of the cut rose flowers.

b) The survey results on the experimental rose plant revealed the following:

People generally thought that the natural rose plants had more diversity and richness compared to the experimental rose plants.

A certain segment of the population who liked cut flowers liked the experimental plants much more because it met their needs of cutting flowers for a variety of purposes such as regular attendance at parties, weddings, offerings at places of worship and so on.

The farmer and his wife were now baffled because they had never faced such a dilemma before in their business. Their son convinced them that by next year the family would double their sales because they could venture into the export market. He was simply looking out for the best interests of the family. The father was confused and so was the daughter. The mother pondered long and hard on the decision, She noticed that the experimental rose plants were shorter, and the roses had crowded out the growth of the leaves and the stems. The stems appeared thinner and shorter. She thought to herself that the consumer really did not like experimental rose plants for this reason. While she knew this was certainly a creative venture on the part of her son, she just couldn't agree with her son to carry on the experiments anymore.

She reasoned that one day they would only be in the business of cut flowers rather than full-grown plants because of the lucrative nature of the export market. However, if the export market had a downturn, she worried how she would get back into the business of selling rose plants. She also felt that the more plants people grew, the better it would be for the environment. She was also afraid that the town would think that she had neglected the neighborhood to cater to a more lucrative market.

Finally, after some soul searching, the family resorted to its old ways. They still retained their customers, continued to grow and serve the community with natural rose plants, and the business continued to boom. However, they never expanded into the foreign markets and capitalize on the additional growth opportunity. But it satisfied them to see that most of their neighbors, friends, and consumers had a thicket of rose plants in their gardens. The farmer and his wife always delighted giving advice on growing and maintaining the plants. Subconsciously, they were relieved that they had never entered the export market because they were simply content helping people. It gave them profound joy and meaning to their lives to see every house with a minimum of one rose plant (Part 2 of the story continues in Chapter 7).

Moral of Part 1 of the Story

If this story has any resemblance to real life, then it is purely coincidental. The moral is that every person in this story had a purpose and everyone was behaving within his assigned role of improving the business. The diversity of the family added strength to the business. Everyone had a unique level of skill sets that contributed to the growth of the business. Without the son building the greenhouse, the young rose plants would have died; without their daughter's help they would have been unable to gauge consumer preferences; without the mother, who knows where the business would have gone. And, yes, the father ensured that the business produced enough plants to satisfy the needs of the customers. The diversity of skill sets in the family kept everything in balance.

The important thing to learn here is that wisdom is sometimes more important than a formal process of education. Therefore, in any entity, corporation, or family, we may want wisdom to take the lead role regardless of which party it emanates from. Hierarchy is not necessarily associated with wisdom. Sometimes people in the lower hierarchy may have more wisdom than people in the higher hierarchy. Sometimes it is the lower culture that benefits the higher culture much more. The great anthropologist Weston La Barre, who collaborated with R.E.Schultes on his early peyote research, wrote of the South American Indian:

"As scientists we can not afford the luxury of an ethnocentric snobbery which assumes a priori that primitive cultures have nothing whatsoever to contribute to civilization. Our civilization is, in fact, a compendium of such borrowing, and it is demonstrable error to believe that contacts of "higher" and "lower" cultures show benefits flowing exclusively in one direction. Indeed, a good case could probably be made that in the long run it is the "higher" culture which benefits the more through being enriched, while the "lower" culture not uncommonly disappears entirely as a result of the contact."

I can never recall reading a case study in my business program in India or, for that matter, even in America, that addressed environmental issues – none whatsoever. My business case studies resembled the story of the young man who was the plant biologist as mentioned in the story above. The case centered more on his life and his aspirations only. I doubt if formal schooling teaches the true essence of diversity. You simply learn this the hard way.

This story will continue to gather a little more momentum as we move forward in the succeeding chapters.

4

Ecology and Human Health

In early 1998, I forayed into the field of writing. I had never written before. I dreaded the thought of writing a book. Who had the time and energy to do such an undertaking? A full-time job, a family, and household chores — all of these factors decreased any motivation to write a book. However, I pulled myself from this languorous state and made a slow start in bits and pieces. Over a four-year period I wrote the book, *Healthcare Reborn: Innovative Essays That Will Lower Costs and Improve Well Being Through Balance and Harmony.*

After I finished writing this book, I felt I was writing more on ecology than on human health. I just could not separate the two. We all know that they are inextricably interlinked. If one were to look at the trajectory of the historical progress of different nations and map them to their disease states, a definite correlation seems to exists. Chronic diseases found in rural China are different that in the chronic diseases found among the rich of any Western country. Within India itself, the chronic diseases within New Delhi are different from those found in the less polluted rural areas. The comfortable sofa we sit on, the car we drive, the shoes we wear, the soap we use, literally anything and everything we touch, feel, wear, and see in this world is not free from toxic material. The sad part of the story is that when all these chemicals enter the production or manufacturing processes they are termed as being hazardous. However, once out of the factory and in the hands of the consumer, no one seems to care or bother since somehow through some miracle they become innocuous. Unfortunately, it is the several countless residues from these products that harm our environment—the leaded fumes from the car, the PVC and volatile organic chemicals from our shoes, the small amounts of antimony from our polyester shirt or dress, the electro-magnetic radiation from our TV, or the dust from our printer toner cartridge, etc. This list can go on. The poem below shows some of my reflections on the link between ecology and human health.

Ecology and Human Health

Don't see health as a distinct problem to be solved,

See health as a pattern of problems.

Open your awareness to unlock the pattern,

The pattern is strewn, stitched, and intertwined.

Locked we are in the embrace of nature,

The land, the sun, the water, and the brisk pure air.

Destroy the forests, we destroy our lungs,

Destroy the land, we destroy our own body,

Destroy the ozone, we destroy our skin,

Pollute the water, we pollute our blood.

The wonderful earth and the species so magnanimous,

The wonderful human, the body within it,

The wonderful body, the cells within it,

All intertwined, interconnected, and so seemingly deceptive,

In their discreet states, they appear so gullible,

Distinct and discrete they get exploited.

Yet so much a part of a checkered pattern,

Seeing problems as discrete, the mind rules over wisdom

As wisdom fails.....

We fail to see patterns as several underlying problems.

For alas, the health of the human microcosm mirrors

The health of the cosmic macrocosm,

One lives not without the other.

The very word physician is derived from the Greek *physis* meaning "nature", and in this neglected fact is the core of a healing secret. While human beings have forgotten the connection between ecology and human health, fortunately, instinct has programmed animals with an inherent knowledge of medicinal plants that our own species is now again beginning to appreciate and study. Monkeys use plants for their medicinal properties, such as to kill parasites. Elephants in Kenya may consume a tree to induce labor, and the women of Wa Tongwe in Kenya, Africa also use the very same plant to induce labor or abortion. Ethnobotanist Mark Plotkin cites several such examples in his book, *Medicine Quest: In Search of Nature's Hidden Cures*. In a Reuters telephone interview, he remarked, "I'm sick and tired of hearing people say conservation is a rich man's game, that it is anti-people or anti-business. If you're not concerned about cancer and AIDS and drug-resistant bacteria, may be you shouldn't be interested in conservation. But there are concrete examples of (conservation's) dollar worth and potential."[2]

5

The Population Dilemma

The books of Paul Ehrlich and Anne Ehrlich prompted me to ask one simple question that probably everyone has wondered at one time or another: "Why does India have such a high population?" I did not find any one answer. The best answer and solution to the population problem was revealed in an article, "In the Footsteps of Gandhi – An Interview With Vandana Shiva." The article was part of a radio series, "Insight & Outlook" hosted by Scott London.[1] Although I never read Vandana Shiva's books (other than some interviews), I thought she was like a modern-day ecological pundit. Her opinion on the population problem is that high population is the result of an ecological phenomenon of displacement. This is an opinion I personally endorse. However, I also feel that we should keep in mind several other factors with respect to free will, individual responsibility, and accountability for our own actions.

While my poem is a common man's perception on population, it certainly expanded my thinking on what Vandana meant. Her interview gave me the courage to think in this expanded dimension.

Ram Ramprasad

The Population Dilemma

Population, Population, Population,

Teeming numbers, teeming millions,

We hit the billion mark at the turn of the century,

Who knows where we are headed.

The planners sharpen their pencils sharp,

Getting to the drawing board with yet another grandiose plan,

Program after program the pundits talk,

Ever implementing each one with a renewed zeal.

What works and what doesn't,

Is never to be asked.

Who knows why we reproduce thus,

The underlying psychology is nobody's guess.

What makes a man and a woman want more,

Destitute and decrepit, we still multiply.

Tools, programs, campaigns, and contraceptives,

Do they ever work?

What works is not one thinks works,

What works is what we think will never work.

The true Gandhi's know what works and what doesn't.

Let liberty, freedom, and justice fill the air.

Let equality banish caste and creed,

Let freedom security, and free speech sail through unfettered.

Let us love each one as we love ourselves.

Hindu, Muslim, Sikh, Christian, Buddhist, Jew, or Jain.

Let us see homogeneity in diversity,

And diversity in homogeneity.

Neither education, nor intellect, nor superiority will uplift us,

Wisdom, respect, and love alone will contain the teeming numbers.

Love not just the human species,

Love all species: human, plant, insect or animal.

Programs, Programs, Programs,

Let's forget about them.

I end this chapter with a quote from *State of World Population 2001*, a report by the United Nations Population Fund (UNFPA):

"Today every part of the natural and human world is linked to every other. Local decisions have a global impact. Global policy, or the lack of it, affects local communities and the conditions in which they live. Humans have always changed and been changed by the natural worlds; the prospects for human development now depend on our wisdom in managing the relationship; one of the key factors will be population. It is also one of the areas where actions to broaden choice is universally available, affordable and agreed upon."[2]

6

Definition of Growth

Even with the high growth of the population in India, I feel the country is still engrossed in a problem that escapes common imagination. While our ecosystems get totally destroyed and plundered, we still seem to encourage a culture that is depleting nature. One wonders how long we can sustain a linear growth attitude at the expense of nature.

Current Definition Of Growth

The Checkbook of the world is damned too puzzling,

The more we tap into nature...

Our material assets increase, but our spiritual assets decrease,

Our health liabilities increase, but our ecosystem resources decrease.

What, we yet foster.....

Is to tap evermore to increase our material assets.

And, yet it becomes nature's responsibility to replenish itself,

With sophisticated global arbitrage and cash flow financing.

We exacerbate what we want to contain,

And we contain what we want to exacerbate.

We create world forums' and exchange intellectual opinions,

We create trade bodies and foster more growth.

Like the dog chasing its tail, we wonder what is wrong

We create an enigma, to resolve an enigma.

We delight in the game...

After all, it increases our GNP

We created the best economic tool in this world,

Assets plus our natural liabilities equal our GNP

The higher the number, the better off we are,

The little flickering sparks to replenish nature...

Get drowned in the less-known voice of the non-profit corporations,

We dance in merriment, and trepidate on a self-created natural calamity,

We address the calamity and increase our GNP

We think we are progressing while silently regressing.

The reports show an ever-glowing statistics,

Of our state in Xanadu, when the reality is dichromatic.

Perhaps most people would question the insight provided above. But I am not alone in this race. The *Global Environment Outlook 2000*, published by the United Nations Environment Programme (UNEP) in its opening section on "Global Perspectives" has the following statement: "A significant proportion of humanity still lives in dire poverty, and projected trends are for an increasing divergence between those that benefit from economic and technological development, and those that do not. This unsustainable progression of extremes of wealth and poverty threatens the stability of society as a whole, and with it the global environment."[1]

Pachamama: Our Earth, Our Guture,[2] is a special youth edition of UNEP's *Global Environmental Outlook 2000.*

Created as a global environment primer for 11- to 14-year olds, the book was launched in late 1999. *Pachamama* (a word meaning Mother Earth in the Inca culture) is the product of youth editors, designers, and hundreds of young contributors worldwide, with the support of UNEP and Peace Child International. UNESCO and UNICEF were also project partners. The book's young editors warn readers that, if they behave as recklessly as their parents, "the good ship Planet Earth will crash sometime in the not too distant future." "We don't have an environmental problem," they add, "We have social, economic and political problems that greatly affect our environment."

The 96-page book contains information, case studies, games, and topics for classroom discussion of major environmental issues, ranging from atmospheric and fresh water problems to urbanization and the protection of polar areas. It is complemented by two companion publications, a teacher's guide and suggestions for taking action – including a "how-to" guide for reaching political leaders.

In a survey of 10,000 youth, the environment and associated problems were most often cited as earth's most pressing priority, followed by human rights, education, and health. Environmental concerns ranked among the top four youth priorities in 44 countries, including the U.K., Japan, the United States, Canada, the Philippines, Sri Lanka, Vietnam, South Africa, Uganda, Jordan, Kuwait, Norway, Belgium, Finland, Spain, Ukraine, Belarus, Bolivia, Peru, Ecuador, and Australia.

Top Environmental Trends are covered in a section entitled "What Scientists Say." *Pachamama* looks into the future and presents the consensus of 200 international experts (canvassed by UNEP for GEO-2000) who put climate change and freshwater scarcity at the top of a 24-point list of key 21st century environmental issues.

Juxtaposed with the scientific consensus is the collective view of 10,000 youth surveyed during *Pachamama's* preparation, who say the world's top 10 positive and negative emerging environmental issues and trends are:

Top 10 negative trends:

- Increased pollution
- Worse water pollution
- More deforestation
- Water scarcity
- Intensified hunting of animals
- More toxic waste
- More air pollution
- Overpopulation
- Widening ozone hole
- Increased amounts of rubbish

Top 10 positive emerging trends

- Increased recycling
- Higher environmental awareness
- More reforestation
- More measures against pollution
- Greater animal protection
- More power to NGOs
- More use of solar energy
- More natural food products
- Water conservation
- More protection of rainforests

Klaus Toepfer, Executive Director of UNEP, calls *Pachamama* "an inspired, sometimes frightening, collection of case studies, poems and drawing to tell the story of our global environment. Some things (Youth) have to say are disturbing—adults have acted irresponsibly in caring for the environment. But young people are also enthusiastically dedicated to their future – a future where Mother Earth is healthy and where people work together to solve our current and future problems."

The current divergence in economic policies largely designed by adults is so incongruent with the wisdom of the world's youth that it is quite embarrassing. Since 1950, the global economy has more than quintupled in size, yet the negative trends are more pronounced than the positive trends. Therefore, the definition of growth needs to be viewed in the right perspective while one-quarter of the worlds' population still remains in abject poverty.[3]

7

The Dilemma of Economics

Yes, poetry, or the theorization that it brings, can be confusing. So, let us take a pause and return to story telling. Remember, the story of Zindabad from Chapter 3. Well, Part 2 of the story continues below:

The Story of Zindabad (Part 2 of 4)

For 20 years, the business of Mr. and Mrs. Gulab Raja prospered. As they reached their late 60s, they no longer wanted to continue with the business. They handed the full reins of the business to their son, Gulab Raja, Jr, Being an ambitious entrepreneur, he soon quit his scientific position as a teacher. He immediately went back to his passion for experiments and recreated new rose plants that had almost 30 roses for every one leaf. He stopped selling rose plants to the local community. He hired some bright business graduates and expanded his business overseas. The government of Zindabad was extremely happy with his efforts because he brought the much-needed foreign exchange to their country. With this money, he further forayed into establishing huge chemical plants.

The city of Zindabad had a huge beautiful lake of a little more than a mile in diameter, the Asli Pani Lake. The government had established an industrial park around this lake; many other small enterprises also started flourishing around this lake. The lake was very popular with the local fishermen, numbering close to over 100. They caught fresh fish and their wives used to sell the fish in different parts of the township. The fishermen, through their expert local knowledge, developed good breeding practices and kept in balance the optimal amount of fish caught versus the amount they used to breed in the lake. A self-appointed local fish chief assured that this balance was never upset. However, the balance was disrupted as industries were built around Asli Pani Lake.

The integrity of the lake was further compromised when industrial effluents were being dumped into this lake. There were no local environmental laws to protect this practice. The children from local schools and colleges who used to learn swimming in Asli Pani Lake slowly stopped for fear of bad health. Over time, mosquitoes populated the lake, using the water as their breeding ground. The government of Zindabad wanted to be a premier State to encourage industry and hence gave permission to several other industries to cut down trees and forests and build more factories. The monkeys that used these small forests as their abode now escaped their habitat and started roaming around the city of Zindabad. They became a nuisance in most neighborhoods. With the growth in industry, the people of Zindabad stopped growing their rose plants. They just didn't have the time and Gulab Raja Jr's nursery would not sell any more rose plants because he was exporting roses to the Middle East. Also, the people of Zindabad were now being paid higher for salaried jobs in the industrial park, so they had to get up early and drive their cars to work. They simply had no time to grow rose plants.

Realizing the mosquito problem, three new companies opened up in the industrial park manufacturing repellant creams, coils, buzzers, etc., so that it kept the mosquitoes away from the houses of the people of Zindabad. This generated more employment in the industrial park. Soon, the auto manufacturers realized the potential for cars in the Zindabad city and wooed many customers to buy cars with special financing schemes. The traffic continued to increase and the commute time increased from 15 minutes to almost one hour in a decade.

With the increase in commute time, people did not have time to cook. Therefore, more new companies started round Asli Pani lake to manufacture packaged food products. With the constant increase in industry, the levels of pollution slowly started to choke the township. Most of the population in the Zindabad township started suffering from asthma. New industries were again established in the industrial park to address this new phenomena of health that now seemed so rampant.

In the meantime, most of the local fishermen had lost their jobs because there were no fish to catch in the Asli Pani lake. The fishermen's wives stayed home and so did the husbands because their skills were now no longer marketable. They were angry at their plight. But to whom should they complain? These displaced families began to have more children They felt that the larger their number, the better they would be able to fight back. A research analyst with a degree in physics and ecology published this peculiar phenomena of population growth due to ecological displacement in a scientific journal. But, then, who reads all those scholarly journals? So the efforts of the researcher went completely ignored by the media.

While all this was happening, economists and statisticians used the Zindabad city as a model for economic growth. They had more industry. The Zindabad government, with the foreign exchange it earned, also embarked on cleaning up the Asli Pani lake after some protests from concerned folks. To the surprise of the government, the cleaning up of the lake further increased the GNP of the township. Zindabad was touted in most newspapers as the model for economic growth. People in the Middle East who received rose flowers on a regular basis from Zindabad paid glowing tributes to the city and Gulab Raja, Jr.

Most economists touted Zindabad as a model economy that transformed itself from an agrarian society to a highly industrialized society. Everyone had a car, the surround sound music systems now replaced the chirping birds which used to visit the rose trees of all the houses in Zindabad. So what if people were suffering from asthma and pollution, there were now modern medicines and electronic air filtration gadgets to address this issue. Most physicians convinced the population that this was normal everyday occurrence and they should learn to live with it. After all, business magazines never addressed ecology. These voices belonged only to the minority and their voices were quite subdued. Therefore , the population accepted everything as given since these changes were taking place incrementally and almost went unnoticed, i.e. the increase in pollution, the increase in traffic, the mosquitoes, the slow changes in the climate due to the pollution, asthmatic conditions, and other detriments.

If this story has any resemblance to reality, then it is purely coincidental. It is this story that led me to wonder on the dilemma of economics.

The Dilemma of Economics

Ever-overwhelming problems,

Ever-overwhelming solutions,

Aiming for quantum leaps in quantum mathematical modeling,

Treating at most times, the "effect" and not the "cause"

Resulting yet in another "Top-Down" fix,

When "Bottom-Up" is one way to fathom the cause and effect,

Interest Rate and Income Taxes... are they all Top-Down?

Does economics address depletion of nature?

How about a tax on consumption for products that deplete nature?

No, we dare not turn economics upside down, It tilts and makes straight-line economics go topsy-turvy.

Which analytical system is the best:

"Top-Down" planning or a "Bottom-Up" planning

One may concentrate power in a few hands,

One may distribute power in several hands.

What does economics seek:

The benefit of all or the benefit of a few?

There is no conclusion for this part of the story. Gulab Raja, Jr. in his mind thought he was doing the right thing. Yes, he was sending effluents into the lake. But did anyone tell him this was wrong? Or was his conscience trained enough to discern between what was right and wrong? Did he have any training on the impact effluents could have on ecosystems? Yes, one should know this quite intuitively. After all, it is common sense. We also go to business schools to learn common sense.

Perhaps we can hold a grudge against Gulab Raja, Jr. Maybe some were unsettled by his unconventional tinkering with the rose plants. But the people in the Middle East were very happy with him. He believed he was doing right by providing employment and creating jobs. New industries started to address the newly created problems. Somehow the excess growth of the population seemed to get absorbed into this industry as well. The government and citizens after all were creating jobs and employing people.

Then what really went wrong in this story? This is the question we need to ask ourselves. If Gulab Raja, Jr. were educated via informal methods of training along with the formal methods would he have behaved differently? The answer is more likely rather than less likely. Why didn't the government enact laws to take care of the pollution? They just could not foresee these problems; they felt it was not their responsibility. Even if they created new laws, they believed the laws would be too hard to enforce.

Therefore, we keep getting into this vicious circle of a blame game. Place the problems of Zindabad on a magnified scale such as the world. This is what makes the issues of the world so complex. This is why the focus on education and on ecosystem literacy becomes so important. Reintroduction of a non-formal approach to education may be the key to good development. Such education was entrusted by the family to the children years ago. Non-formal schooling in consciousness-based education was a way of life. However, this practice is not so common any more. Therefore, the onus falls on the educational institutions. We need systems of education that are formal, nonformal, and a hybrid of both. Individuals need not wait for the government to do everything; they can take this up on their own. Markets are always built on human need; if individuals desire it, the institutions will start automatically. Nothing is accomplished overnight; everything in the world is a slow process. But, if we do not make a start, we never will get anywhere.

8

Education Methods — The Crux of the Problem

From the previous chapter, one can only ponder and conclude that real solutions will always lie with the system of our education. Education and youth are the future to any country's long-term stability. While diversity needs full encouragement, we should not forget the philosophical basis of education. Education needs to be holistic with equal emphasis on the body, the mind, and the soul. Developing a monoculture in education develop only a monocultural economy.

Education – Reflections on an Approach

In a sheer ecstatic dilemma, I asked myself a quixotic question...

What is education?

Is education of the soul more important than the education of the mind?

The more I pampered my mind, the more joy it gave my senses;

The more joy my senses achieved, the more pain I felt.

The philosopher Henri Bergson once said;

"The intellect is characterized by a natural inability to know life."

Then, what is education?

The formal school I attended, or the non-formal school that life is.

I flinched at the assault of technology on nature,

Or, did I flinch at the assault of man on the way he utilized technology.

I vacillated and waffled and perhaps blamed both,

I still couldn't attribute consciousness to the non-conscious things around me.

I felt passing the world like a voyeur, lonely and without purpose.

Perhaps we all felt the same one time or another.

We simply seem to amass degrees and sail on with life,

We keep writing thesis after thesis.

We tend to master the obscure and forget the obvious.

There was a time when we developed simple solutions to complex problems.

Now, we develop complex solutions to simple problems.

How else will the education and the satellite industries survive.

Swami Vivekananda once said:

"All knowledge exists in this world, we are only uncovering it."

Gravity always existed, Newton just discovered it.

The world is a theory and not a problem.

Discover the theory and you discover the problem.

In a fleeting moment, I remembered Tagore.

As he put it:

"Emancipation from the bondage of the soil is not freedom for the tree."

The tumultuous waves in my mind slowly settled,

Thoughts came rushing and pouring in again.

Tagore with his experiment in Shantiniketan,

Swami Vivekananda and his national resurgence through the Ramakrishna Mission,

Sri Aurobindo and his spiritual regeneration,

Mahatma Gandhi on achieving Swaraj,

Didn't this great soul once say,

"True education should result not in material power, but in

Spiritual force"

Education to them meant a "soul-to-soul" interaction,

A real resurgence in villages.

Trepidated they were at Western methods and its

Consequential inequities.

They were for an education that grew our consciousness,

An education that created equity for all without rejecting

Scientific development.

I question myself: Did I learn more from a formal or a

Non-formal education?

Did I gain more wisdom from the epic tales and stories

Written by our great sages?

Or, did I learn more from a one-sided formal education

Skewed towards non-reciprocity?

My mind finally clamed, for I knew formal or non-formal...

All education must rest in understanding the law of reciprocity,

It must rest in understanding more of our conscience rather

Than stuff our intellect.

Our great heritage has promised, the more we focus on the

Ever-conscious soul,

The greater wisdom we will attain.

History, time, heritage, and the great gurus have proven this to be
thus:

Let's dig up the past and liven that ancient glory!

Was it not in the late 1700s that the carpenter was also the

Keeper of the forests,

He knew what wood to cut and chop and what trees to grow.

Trades and professions were seamlessly intertwined in

Melodious reciprocity.

One being's waste became another being's sustenance.

The human and animal species exchange oxygen for carbon dioxide with the plants

Thy flying birds exchange their droppings for the fruit and

Nut of the plants.

History reveals that our professions, trades, and our transactions...

Were all intermingled and married in a joyful dance of reciprocity.

Indeed, this kept even the human numbers in balance with nature

How can our hearts and eyes behold the majestic education

We never saw?

We hear it in the tales, we hear about their existence in the Vedas,

We hear about heir true purity when the pundits quote

From the Upanishads,

Let's open our minds and hearts once again,

Let's redeem the hidden treasure buried in the sands of time.

Wisdom has brought us one step closer,

Come, let's all sail the seas to the yonder lore.

9

A Simple Guide to Sustainable Living

What if we are already educated and if we really think our traditional training does not permit us to live in communion with nature? Well, little attempts are always possible. I think it was Swami Chinmayananda who once said that if you want to embark on a big project do not really start in a big way; simply start in a small way and before you realize, the project itself becomes a major undertaking, in some small measure, this has helped me plan my own work.

Should one then wait to achieve the desired goal of sustainable living that would be less taxing on the environment? Not necessarily. The first step is to believe in possibilities. There are many options to follow in life: in our present job, or even in entrepreneurship. The poem below has some clues. The answers will have to be developed by our own imagination and creativity. However, if we all commit ourselves to a grand vision, living in harmony with nature is possible. Sustainable living is not a dream but a reality that can be fulfilled for now and forever regardless of your chosen profession.

A Simple Guide to Attaining Sustainable Living

I wondered hard what kind of a professional I would make!

I needed to make a living, but without harming society or nature,

Any technology I chose helped society but ruined nature,

But never did I find technology that helped and replenished nature.

But then I came across some wonderful books and wonderful authors,

I urge you to read their works through and through.

The more I read Paul Hawken, Amory Lovins, and Hunter Lovins,

I knew Natural Capitalism was possible.[1]

Yes, there is technology that can power your home,

Clean fuel cell, wind, or solar power; cheaper than the ones you use.

Yes, there is technology that can drive you to work,

Clean fuel-powered bicycles, or a fuel cell autorickshaw.

Why crowd and pollute our roads that were not built for cars?

Yes, there is technology that will not pollute the rivers,

Zero-emission factories or biodegradable plastics.

Yes, there is technology that will not kill trees,

Paper made from hen and chicken feathers.

Yes, there is technology that will even power your home

Without a dam.

The Garlov Helical Turbine produces more power than a

Conventional turbine,[2]

And yet requires no dam.

Yes, there is more than the eye or the heart can behold.

Read the profound writings on Agroecology:

Organic farming or protecting your heritage, it is all on the web.

Or, read Shashikala Ananth for living in harmony with the environment.[4]

More of a disbelief in living in accord with nature.

Then test and challenge yourself to read the books of Dr. Tony Nader.[5]

Armed with degrees from MIT and Harvard, he sets to prove the parallels,

Between the glorious macrocosm and the microcosm,

Doubting always to become a vegetarian or seeking the best

Synthesis between East and West.

Read the book, The Holy Science by Swami Yukteswar.[6]

Why waste time in entrepreneurship that exploits nature,

Waste time in entrepreneurship that replenishes nature.

Linear growth at the expense of nature is just a mirage,

Non-Linear growth that replenishes nature is nourishing

To body, mind, and soul.

Listen to the words of the wise,

Not the minds of the ego-intellect.

We are better off following instinct than reason alone.

The animals lives by instinct alone,

Homing pigeons know their abode and dogs know when

Their masters return home.

Using instinct is not medieval progress,

It balances intellect in wholesome progress

Yes, we often want to fight reason with reason.

Then go ahead and read the book, The Betrayal of Science

And Reason:[7]

A painstaking well-annotated, and a monumental work by

Paul Ehrlich and Ann Ehrlich.

Fight then reason with reason, but fight it right,

Not with ego, not with possessiveness,

But with an attitude to serve, share, and coexist.

Perfection is impossible but sustainable living is simple and possible.

Challenge yourself to grow the conscience and not just the intellect,

The former nourishes, the latter tends to extract and appease the self.

Time again for some storytelling:

The Story of Zindabad (Part 3 of 4)

While Gulab Raja, Jr. was building an industrial empire, his sister Gulab Rani had finished her PhD program in urban planning. After teaching in a local university for a while, she felt she needed a career change and started her own consulting company called Gulab Consultants. The people of Zindabad believed that she was following in the footsteps of her mother. She never took a fragmented approach to any problem; rather she took a systematic approach to analyze problems. She believed in the principle that one being's waste should be another being's sustenance. She believed in the law of reciprocity. Nothing escaped her attention. Her philosophy was based on a more people-centric approach. She believed that if people were given more power, and were empowered, more progress could be achieved in Zindabad.

She had made a deliberate attempt to start a consulting firm because it perturbed her conscience to see the city's deteriorating condition. Using her skills in urban planning, she prepared a master business plan to solve the traffic congestion problem of Zindabad. Being open-minded, she sought the best ideas from every part of the world as well as from the wise peasants in Zindabad. She never let her PhD go to her head.

Gulab Rani studied the urban planning model of Curitiba, a city in Brazil. At professional conferences she had learned that it was a model to be emulated. Curitiba's buses carried two times more passengers than they did 20 years ago, but people spent only about 10 per cent of their yearly income on transport. As a result, despite the second highest per capita car ownership in Brazil (one car for every three people), Curitiba's gasoline use per capita was 30 percent below that of eight comparable Brazilian cities. Other results included negligible emission level, little congestion, and an extremely pleasant living environment.[8] She visited the model city to get a first hand look and used her impressions to fashion a plan for Zindabad.

She also researched fuel cell technology for cars, bicycles, and auto rickshaws. She somehow managed to find a small company that would convert leaded gas to unleaded gas. She developed a plan for Zindabad; to her surprise the government approved it. She was glad that the government was committed to making a difference.

Her next mission was to help people expand their small-scale industrial base. Once, a small poultry farmer approached her. He complained he was wasting all of the chicken and hen feathers. He wanted to know if there was something that could be done with these feathers. She surfed the web and discovered that a small newspaper called *Agricultural Innovation News* in America published several ideas for the small-scale farmer. One of them included converting feathers to paper, polymer films, and biodegradable plastic. She contacted the right sources and through her firm secured the technology for the farmer. As a committed social worker, she disseminated this knowledge to all the poultry farmers in Zindabad.

She also consulted several corn farmers on how to produce biodegradable plastics. The big industries in the industrial park soon started facing severe competition because the small-scale industries supplied their products locally and took advantage of lower freight costs. The local fishermen who were unemployed slowly switched to the business of transporting paper and plastic from the farms to the proximal sources that needed them. The farmers discovered that they could produce their own packaging materials and were happy that Gulab Rani provided them with technologies that gave more power and money to them.

Gulab Rani once came across an article in *The Resurgence*, a magazine founded by Satish Kumar of The Schumacher College in England. The article, "No Waste Economy," was written by Günter Pauli. Günter's solution to the problems of the world was for humans to do more with whatever the earth produces rather than to make the earth produce more.

Gulab Rani loved citing the example of Günter Pauli on the sisal plant. The sisal plant is the number one crop in Tanzania. It is the main crop in Mexico, in Colombia and in Brazil. The sisal plant is used for its fiber, mostly to make ropes. Ships still have sisal ropes. No synthetic rope has the strength of a sisal rope. But the sisal fiber is only 2 percent of the plant, 98 percent is waste. This meant that Tanzania has 11.8 million tones of biomass waste a year dumped into the river. Unfortunately, the Tanzanians were not taking advantage of producing citric acid and lactic acid, natural components produced from the bole of the sisal plant and a key product of the food industry. Sisal fiber costs $200 a ton and citric acid $3,000 a ton and yet this was being wasted.[9]

Gulab Rani urged her clients to think in a nonlinear fashion. She wanted farmers as well as small and large business enterprises to have zero-waste. Therefore, her idea was not to craft a strategy to create a product, but rather create several strategies to take care of the waste that came out of the creation of any one product. She believed that there was more to gain by all parties by closing the ecological cycle. She detested open-ended ecological and environmental systems, and believed in open economic systems. If businesses did not know how to answer the question of closing the ecological and the environmental loop, she figured that such a business model would only increase the cumulative costs to society.

Gulab Rani published an academic paper on the phenomena of equitable wealth distribution as a result of some of the consulting services she provided. An MBA intern conducted a research project on the positive impact of Gulab Consultants to the Zindabad economy. His research did not focus on the growth in the GDP. On the contrary, his research focused on the creation of social capital in the community. For demographers, social capital takes on as much importance as money. The bright intern published his thesis in layman's terms in the regional newspaper. His article explained how Gulab Consultants reduced the commute time for several families, created jobs within their community, lowered the rate of depression, lowered the rate of crime, increased the growth of informal communications, and increased the growth of more social and healthier relationships. The article was well-publicized since it correlated improvement in social capital to improvement in ecological or natural capital. The publicity caused many bright young graduates to clamor for work at Gulab Consultants. Although the pay scales were slightly lower than what the industry provided, some bright graduates saw the shifting patterns and wanted to take their first-mover advantage by joining Gulab Rani's firm.

Professor Bhupati, Dean of the University of Zindabad, was impressed with the article written by the MBA Intern. Ironically, he learned a lot from the article, written by a student of his own university. After a personal conversation with the Intern, Professor Bhupati devised a new education policy for the University of Zindabad. He tried to nurture a movement within the university called "place-based education."

This education theory takes the history, culture, economy, and ecology of a community and uses them as both a textbook and laboratory. He had heard about place-based education on his overseas visits, but it did not mean much to him until he read the article. As soon as the board approved the policy, the local schools also seemed very interested in the concept. Students began working with the community to solve local problems; they got actively engaged in analyzing water samples from creeks to determine the flow of pollutants. Some other students from a different school started restoring a local temple, a mosque, and a church.

Students from the University of Zindabad interviewed local doctors about traditional growing cycles and plant remedies. Some ambitious engineering students adapted fuel cell technology to power auto rickshaws and solar technology to power street lights. A group of engineering students teamed up with a group of life science students to invent a novel meter that would measure the amount of industrial and toxic sludge that left a household's sewer pipes. These ambitious students encouraged the government of Zindabad to replace state taxes with "sludge taxes." The students believed that waste-water treatment plants should only treat biological sludge by natural means to produce natural fertilizer. They had a sincere zeal to improve the population's long-term health.

Another group of biology students consulted local fish and shrimp breeders on the effective use of blue-green algae growing in their ponds. Cyanobacteria or blue-green algae are believed to be the earth's first oxygen-producing organisms and naturally secrete cellulose – an essential component of all sorts of materials, including paper and fabric. Prior to the students' visit, the breeders disposed of gelatinous glue produced by the bacteria. At the students' recommendation the gelatinous glue was turned over to the University of Zindabad for a decent remuneration.

The students began working on a project of converting the glue to paper. They were confident of developing a simple process whereby people would never harvest trees for a paper pulp. The approach of the students was not for fewer blue-green algae to produce more gelatinous glue through gene manipulation; they wanted more people to grow more blue-green algae and thus produce more gelatinous glue. The logic was simple; they wanted the masses employed, and they did not want to disrupt the natural processes of life because they were not certain of the consequences.

For example, they were not certain how gene manipulation would affect the fish, humans, and the environment. One of the biology students encouraged the production of soy ink and made a recommendation to the government. He felt that if all the paper produced from blue-green algae utilized soy ink, it ultimately could be converted to a food additive for the cattle or manure for the trees. This would thus satisfy the criteria of one person's waste becoming another being's food. Once these biology students understood the broader principles of the natural laws of life, they felt the experiments were simple and less cumbersome. All of their experiments were within a broader vision of the overall cycle of ecology. The students were not biologists; they were "system-thinkers."

As more and more students got involved in place-based education, they started interviewing more and more people in the community. They interviewed people from all walks of life; the person who drove the rickshaw; the vegetable peddler; the storekeeper; the housewife; the office worker; the person who begged on the street and the mechanic. All of these people shared a rich history of their personal experiences and everyday problems that plagued society. The students slowly began to realize that these common men and women identified uncommon ideas that were full of wisdom and foresight.

It slowly dawned on Professor Bhupati that the more the students got involved in the community, the greater was their desire to succeed into heir chosen field of profession. Professor Bhupati's newfound emphasis on place-based education was not creating a generation clamoring for the narrow niches of high-paying jobs in big corporations. To the contrary, it created more social capital and a diversity of entrepreneurial ideas in the community. People and youth through a participatory process were developing local solutions to local problems through a "Bottom-Up," approach rather than having a dependence on "Top-Down," solutions from the government or the politicians. Pride of place, community, and heritage were motivating students to learn, excel – and then give back.

The success of "place-based education" soon spurred in the development of several other complementary and innovative experiments. The University of Zindabad opened satellite campuses in several rural areas. Masters and doctoral level students were encouraged in these campuses to undertake "inter-disciplinary team-oriented projects," rather than an "individual research thesis." Professor Bhupati felt that individual research thesis submission at masters or doctoral levels had minimal impact on society and taught students competition rather than cooperation. Therefore, he wanted each one of his students to have a total and a holistic learning experience by working within a group of people with varying backgrounds. The University of Zindabad replaced individual research thesis submissions with team-oriented projects.

Broadly speaking, students of life sciences collaborated with students of earth science. For example, one of the interdisciplinary teams consisted of an agriculturist, a biologist, a physicist, a chemist, an engineer, and a geologist. This team, which worked in one of the satellite campuses in a rural area, developed a unique natural low-cost technology for refrigeration of food products. Farmers could built this natural low-cost refrigeration right in their very own farms through the use of special earthen clay, stone, sand-stone, air pressure technology, airflow technology, sunlight and other natural sources. The student team through their collective skills mimicked nature. This simple invention contributed to saving several lakhs of rupees in post-harvest losses that was normally suffered by the farmers community. A different interdisciplinary team applied similar concepts in building better houses for the farmers. In the torrid tropical heat, these houses provided natural refrigeration without emitting the chlorofluorocarbons' (CFCs) that were so common with the modern systems of refrigeration.

While all of this was taking place, another interdisciplinary team, mostly consisting of students from the liberal arts fields, studied the slow and steady effects of reverse migration patterns from urban to rural areas in Zindabad. The students noticed that the reverse migration pattern decreased the number of slum dwellers in the urban areas of Zindabad and lowered the levels of pollution. Reverse migration also indirectly contributed to a positive impact in the post-harvest losses in food production since less food and water were transported from rural to urban areas, and there was a general increase in the levels of nutrition and wealth.

Professor Bhupati advised project supervisors to grade the interdisciplinary projects not simply on the resulting impact to the community, but rather to base them on the wisdom and foresight shown by each project team. Interpersonal skills and cooperation amongst and between team members were also criteria used to determine grades. Typical characteristics representative of a modern education system, such as competition, aggressiveness, and dominance, were replaced with team spirit, cooperation, sharing of knowledge, symbiotic learning, and other social skills.

The University of Zindabad slowly scrapped all standardized testing procedures. The administrators believed that these tests only encouraged the development of one-dimensional personalities. The University of Zindabad also changed its recruiting practices and began recruiting people from diverse backgrounds to join the teaching staff. The administrators chose teachers who had a variety of experience in the industry as well as in teaching, spirituality, holistic sciences, and arts. The public perception was that all activities that emanated from the University of Zindabad had a foundation in arts, culture, ecology, and spirituality.

The University of Zindabad did not adopt any product or concept simply because it appeared glamorous on the surface. Every concept and product needed to pass the test of wisdom on what was most appropriate for the society, the community, the environment, the ecology, and the overall well-being of life as it existed in the abode called "mother earth." In his spare time, Professor Bhupati wrote short poems, he would occasionally, put one on a plaque and hang it on the university walls to help constantly remind the students the mission of the university.

One of the plaques contained the following poem:

Alter not the biosphere,

For it is just a delicate shell.

Alter not the dance of biology,

For it is just the very basis of our livelihood and ecology.

Let our missteps not rock and shock the world,

Let our steps teach the world.

Let eco-creativity precede all creative intelligence,

For mother earth says this hath our sustenance.

Professor Bhupati was amazed at the speed and enthusiasm on the execution of several new policies and innovative experiments. He urged several other universities to make the community their classroom instead of wasting resources on projects that had no impact on the community or environment. Professor Bhupati replaced a "publish or perish" monoculture with a plethora of new experiments in education. Professor Bhupati was personally committed to creating more vibrancy in the community. He believed this commitment was better than spending time on scholarly research which had little impact on the community. He stopped using economic models to help convince people of the vibrancy of the Zindabad community. Rather, he encouraged people to shadow his students and learn everything first-hand. Assessing the vibrancy of a community, he felt, was like appreciating natural beauty.

The University of Zindabad started offering courses and choices in several elective subjects. Prior to the concept of "place-based education" and interdisciplinary team projects, the University of Zindabad was only churning out a multitude of experts in very specific disciplines such as medicine, engineering, and law. Most were underemployed since the economics of demand and supply did not seem balanced. As the concept of "place-based education" and several other innovative experiments came into vogue, people realized that there was more employment in "cleaning-up" and similar activities that related to naturalizing the more harmful technologies. Students would sometimes visit websites, such as www.eco-web.com (Green Pages – The Global Directory for Environmental Technology) to keep themselves abreast of job opportunities in these fields or to simply understand what was happening in the different parts of the world with respect to the industrial landscape on environmental technology.

Zindabad began to face a severe power shortage. The government embarked on building a new hydroelectric dam that would cost several crores of rupees. They approached Gulab Rani, she researched the most appropriate means of solving the power crisis in Zindabad. She did not recommend dam construction because the Gorlov Helical turbine that was invented by Dr. Andrew Gorlov was 30 percent more effective than a conventional turbine and did not require the building of a dam. The helical turbine operated in free flowing water.[10] Gulab Rani, with the help of the University of Zindabad, convinced the Zindabad government that this was the right approach because a hydroelectric dam would cause a great amount of ecological damage and would displace several thousand families. She also provided proof on how it might increase the growth in population.

For the apartment dwellers of Zindabad, she recommended that clean fuel cells be installed on top of the apartment complexes. She had also developed a plan for wind power and solar roof panels where several small-scale entrepreneurs could make a big difference. Through a distributed approach for power supply she ensured employment for people and stayed true to her belief of doing the least possible harm to the environment.

The media, who in the past had praised and lauded the work of Gulab Raja Jr, were now praising the work of Gulab Consultants. They took a keen interest in environmental issues. Gulab Rani had essentially salvaged the government's reputation. In appreciation, the government recommended her for a high-level economic position at the central level.

The success of Gulab Consultants soon became a case study in most business schools. The staff of Gulab Consultants included a diverse group of people split equally among men and women, young and old. On the staff were: two physicians; a biologist; an ecologist; an environmentalist; two information systems specialists; two chemists; two physicists; two journalists; two accountants; two business graduate; three engineers of different specialties; and one 68-year-old specialist in informal education. People worked on a flexible schedule. Gulab Rani was not a timekeeper; she just believed in getting the job done. However, Tuesdays were mandatory for everyone to be in the office. All staff brainstormed on every project on this day. Each member of the team got a chance at least once to be a project team leader.

The brainstorming sessions attracted the most attention from the media. Prior to every session, the 68-year-old informal specialist (fondly nicknamed Kakaji) used to advise team members to meditate. All methods were secular. It was simply a process of inner introspection in silence. As a member of the team, he believed answers to solutions were derived both in silence and in healthy debate. He reasoned that most good ideas for most great people were born in silence. It was simple logic and other team members did not deny the wisdom of his approach. Most people were so busy that they found immense relief in this 15-minute silence. It always seemed that he communicated with other members of his team during this silence. After the end of the entire brainstorming session, he spoke for no more than two or three minutes. Most of his team members discussed their most problematic situations with him. He was considered to be the silent leader on all projects.

Gulab Rani's management style was to apply whole systems thinking on any project. Her projects did not address a specific problem but rather took into account the entire ramification surrounding the project. She borrowed the best concepts from both the East and the

West, and then added her own unique creativity to address these problems. While her competitors and other large companies had mixed feelings about her approach, no one could deny that her staff's productivity was twofold that of the average firm. Clients of Gulab Consultants were impressed that any one of the team members could talk at length on any subject. Gulab Rani had secretly created in her brainstorming meetings a symbiosis of matter, mind, and spirit through building a a diverse staff. People on her team were whole-system thinkers, not people who thought in silos or just became "lifers" in a company perhaps doing the same job like assembly-line workers.

Gulab Raja, Jr. was envious of his sister's success and once remarked to her that without his contribution to the foreign exchequer, she wouldn't have accomplished all the collaborative projects from various parts of the world. She responded that she had saved the Zindabad government 80 percent of its revenues on the importation of oil over a five-year period. From these savings, she intended to use no more than five percent of the money for her projects. She dealt with her brother's impetuosity in a placid manner.

Conclusion of the Story

People are confused on when and how to collaborate with overseas countries. Most often we collaborate on the wrong areas or with the wrong parties. As a result, we end up blaming the country instead of the nature of our collaboration. We end up blaming technology when, in the first place, we did not know how to get the best from the rest of the world. We plagiarize products when we need to adapt the most appropriate and applicable concept. Glorious for-profit and not-for-profit institutions exist in every country of the world. It all depends on using the right wisdom for collaboration. Gulab Rani's approach was to first explore local talent before she ventured overseas. She visited a model city and applied whole-systems thinking to both her business and the solutions it provided.

While the story is fictional, the fuel cell technology, the paper from chicken feathers or blue-green algae, the Gorlov Helical turbine, the story of Curitiba, the story of the sisal fiber, the story of Gunter Pauli, the concepts of social capital and "place-based education," are all real or exist in different parts of the world in some shape or form. However, the concept of interdisciplinary team project at masters and doctoral levels and the creation of a device that measures toxic sludge are original ideas. The diagnosis lies in the nature of cooperation between the East and the West. Each sometimes blames the other for its faults. No one country can blame the other, except itself. Every nation created its own laws and executes those laws, Laws exist to protect society, yet laws and taxes do not exist to protect nature. This in itself has been the inadequacy of all systems all over the world. We send a person to prison for life when he murders someone. But we do not have a law for protecting our plant and animal species. Yes, perhaps we have watered down laws on game reserves and animal cruelty. We have simply failed to understand the underlying dynamics on how the world reeds to function. This opinion is reflected below:

East and West — Achieving Perfection by Understanding Imperfection

The Eastern world so expressive inward,

The Western world so expressive outward.

The Eastern world gives a nod and a twinkle to express a Thank you,

The Western world uses glowing words to express a Thank You,

The Eastern world sometimes feels empty on the outside but is happy inside,

The Western world appears happy outside but sometimes feels empty inside.

The Eastern world shows no urgency of time,

The Western world gets excitable with time.

The Eastern world tends to walk to its destination,

The Western world tends to run to its destination.

The Eastern world is less excited with novelty,

The Western world gets excited with novelty.

The Eastern world tries to catch up with an economic race,

The Western world wants to win the economic race.

The Eastern world gets trapped in plagiarizing the race,

The Western world gets trapped in the materialization of the race.

The Eastern world acts to create equity but creates inequity,

The Western world succumbs to creating equity through inequity.

The Eastern world articulates world debates with less polish,

The Western world articulates world debates with great polish.

The Eastern world is aware of the jigsaw puzzle,

Ram Ramprasad

The Western world sees the jigsaw piece.

The Eastern world tries imperfect technology and destroys nature,

The Western world tries to race in technology and thus ruins nature.

The Eastern world feels displaced in their habitat,

The Western world feels they conquered their habitat.

As a consequence, the Eastern world multiplies their breed,

As a consequence, the Western world expands corporate empires.

The Eastern world leaves most ecosystem jobs undone,

The Western world leaves most ecosystem jobs half-done.

The Eastern world relishes quality in human interaction,

The Western world relishes quality in TV interaction.

The Eastern world tries to plagiarize the West,

The Western world believes that a monoculture is the sure

Path to global progress.

The Eastern world has the same interior core as the West,

The Western world has the same interior core as the East.

The Eastern world is akin to the Right Hemisphere of the brain,
The Western world is akin to the Left Hemisphere of the brain.

Therefore, the Eastern world is adept at:
Pattern & spatial recognition, non-verbal ideation, emotional
and parallel processing of information.
Therefore, the Western world is adept at:
Language, Math, Logic, and Processing
Of serial sequences of information

With each hemisphere responsible for the opposite half of the body,
How oblivious we have become of our world body?
Let East seek the best in its strength,
Let West seek the best in its strength.

Like the right hemisphere, let East influence the West,
Like the left hemisphere, let West influence the East.
Progress is not plagiarizing imperfection,
Progress is realizing inherent local talent and strength.
The more we understand the conscience behind the human body.

The more we will understand the conscience of the world body.

Peace, Peace, Peace ... let peace prevail on earth.

The poem above begs to answer the question: Is it Capitalism or Communism? What is really right for humanity? Each system is a man-created system. Therefore each system is fraught with both pros and cons. Most of the time the pros are taken for granted and more easily adopted, while the cons languish behind. We are good at addressing the pros but we seldom want to address the cons. Since concentration on the cons seldom occurs, imperfections begin to arise in each system. The poem below reflects these phenomena.

Capitalism Versus Communism

The way the world goes...

Common men, uncommon ideas,

Uncommon men, common ideas.

Common men generally lost in sloth and labor,

Uncommon men generally lost in domination and control,

Common men left with less proportionate benefit,

Uncommon men left with disproportionate benefit,

Common men get ruled,

Uncommon men rule.

Communism and Capitalism ever so different and ever so same,

One creates the uncommon bureaucrat,

The other one a corporate autocrat.

Neither serves the common man.

The uncommon man mired in paralytic cathexis,

The common man striving for catharsis.

What Capitalism seeks, communism ignores,

What Communism seeks, capitalism ignores,

One chases economy the other chases equity,

But none chases ecology.

What a funny and a deprecating world we live in,

We go round and round in circles,

Creating inequities in health and wealth.

Common man, exalt yourself to a sane uncommonality,

Uncommon man, exalt yourself to a sane commonality,

Let's walk straight with equity and humility.

Both capitalism and communism have created several inadequacies in this world. What we need in this world is a system thinking that can be applied to the study of the multiple relationships that interlink the members of the earth household. Fritjof Capra, an internationally known physicist and the author of several international best sellers such as *The Tao of Physics* and *The Turning Point,* calls these principles the basic facts of life. He recommends that children be taught the following fundamental facts of life:

- That an ecosystem generates no waste, one species' waste is another species' food;
- That matter cycles continually through the web of life;
- That the energy driving these ecological cycles flows from the sun;
- That diversity assures resilience;
- That life, from its very beginning more than three billion years ago, did not take over the planet by combat but by cooperation, partnership and networking.

Fritjof recommends that teaching such knowledge is an ancient wisdom and considers this the most important role of education in this century.[11]

10

Buckling up to Restore Our Ecosystem

One bright Saturday morning while enjoying the ginger tea that my wife made, I browsed through the News India-Times newspaper. An article written by Darryl D'Monte caught my eye. He wrote about an international workshop for environmental journalists in Mumbai. In this meeting, Ramachandra Guha, an environmental historian, put forward a case for academics to turn occasionally to journalism, which would enable them to communicate more frequently and to wider audiences. Research papers and books,by their very nature, take time to complete and don't often reach the masses. D'Monte pointed out that several researchers, including Guha, used the media with distinction.[1]

I ruminated over the article for sometime and reflected on the excellent point that Guha had made. It is likely there are several thousands of researchers capturing the panoramic view of the grass-root struggles being waged by common people against the destruction of their natural resource base. I read names such as P.Sainath and Mukul Sharma and marveled at the amount of work they do, whether it is setting up fellowship for rural development journalism or just capturing the struggle of these movements. Their attitude is what I would like to describe as simply buckling up and doing something that no one has dared to do. People like these give us strength.

Buckling Up

Oh Thou Scientist,

Oh Thou Professional,

Roll up your sleeves,

Show us your work through simple means,

Convey your thoughts in simple streams.

The teacher in the school or the professor in the university,

Explore nature and life in the midst of all its diversity.

The student in the school or the young adult in college,

Walk to the closest library and expand thy knowledge,

Technology is not good or bad,

It is how we use it that makes its plight sad,

The birds, the bees, the flowers, and the trees,

All carry on their lives the simple way,

Perhaps watching them will teach us not to go astray.

It is never too late to make a start,

For, after all, life can act smart,

Buckle up, Buckle up, Buckle up,

Start doing something and you will become that,

Start writing and you will become a writer,

Grow a tree and you will become a tree planter,

Start a business and you will become a businessman,

Start assisting a referee and you will become a linesman,

Go offbeat, start a non-formal college, and you become a pioneer,

Yes, it is never too late to be in a different career.

Here are some additional things one can do on a everyday basis for sustainable living and for buckling up:

- Decide not to litter
- Decide to use recycling programs wisely.
- Stop complaining about the politicians; instead look for ways where you could have be the facilitator instead of the government. This attitude may provide you with an idea to help build your own business.

While reading the book, *Natural Capitalism* by Amory Lovins and Paul Hawkins, I came across information on how a chemistry professor at the University of Zurich started a program to teach his students how to convert toxic wastes into chemical reagents;[2] whereas, many other universities in the world teach how to convert chemical reagents into toxic wastes. If you were to explore the web site, you will find a lot of information on things like green chemistry and how to start an eco-village or an eco-hotel.

The next time you check out at the grocery store, pack your food in a reusable cloth grocery sack. Life is all about building the critical mass. It takes a few people in the neighborhood to care for the environment, and then the enthusiasm spreads like wildfire. Finally, just think differently. Think of the little steps you can take to create something big, something sustaining for future generations. This is what buckling-up and sustainable living is all about.

The Story of Zindabad (Part 4 of 4)

It was March 1, 2015 when Gulab Rani was offered a high-level ministerial position at the Central Government. Relutantly, she decided to leave her position at Gulab Consultants. She made Kakaji, the 68-year-old, informal specialist, the head of Gulab Consultants. He had complete freedom to do what he liked with the company.

Kakaji did not waste time. He immediately gave a stirring speech to colleagues about his decision not to expand the operations of Gulab Consultants. He decided to close the company officially as a business entity. He felt it had served its purpose. He lectured that the very essence of power lies in disseminating the power they had acquired. He quoted the sayings of various gurus. He told his colleagues that it was not all about technology revolutionizing everyone's lives to give them happiness. On the contrary, it was about how all lives in Zindabad would revolutionize technologies. He wanted his colleagues to teach all people the essence of reconnecting, reestablishing, and reconciling their relationships with all living systems – plants, humans, and animals. He wanted each one of them to follow the callings of their hearts.

He told them that the continuation of Gulab Consultants would not benefit the society of Zindabad. On the contrary, he urged each staff member to go his own way, believing the benefit would be much more substantial. He sincerely felt that the accumulated wisdom of each one of them over the years now needed a process of transference to the common man. The speech moved his colleagues and they supported his decision.

Kakaji opened his own Yoga Centre. Schools and colleges were in dire need of informal teachers. He was in the business of meeting these needs. Two of the biologists started breeding dolphins in the Asli Pani lake and entertained people with the antics of the dolphins. These chirpy bright ambassadors bridged the passion of earthlings to the passion of the life in water. One of the engineers created a novel technique of converting organic waste matter to compost manure for home use in kitchen gardening.

The agriculturist entered his own business on advising households on growing kitchen gardens. He had a simple message for farmers and households. "Keep your garden similar to a forest. Does a forest require any maintenance?" When the common man did not understand his simple philosophy, he elaborated, "The forest, my friends, is like a family. The big trees are the father and the mother; their roots penetrate deep into the bowels of the earth and extract the rich nutrients and the minerals of the earth. They then bring this nutrient-rich food to their leaves. When the leaves fall, the small trees and plants feed from them. Just like a strong family does not depend on external support, a strong forest, garden, or a farm does not need the kind of support you may be thinking of."

He advised people to have a diversity of species; he constantly told the farmers that it is the mixed species of plants that foiled pests. He dissuaded the use of fossil fuel-based, manufactured fertilizers and instead preached organic farming methods. For people who lacked space, he developed a unique method of growing kitchen gardens on rooftops. During his spare time, the agriculturist wrote a column in the regional local language newspaper titled, "Agriculture and Horticulture Matters." His column was based on his personal experience with plants as well as providing a commentary on the work of world-renowned horticulturist Luther Burbank.

Luther Burbank (1849 – 1926) was an American horticulturist, botanist, and plant breeder who developed more than 800 strains and varieties of plants, including 113 varieties of plums and prunes, 10 varieties of berries, as well as several varieties of lilies and the Freestone peach. He was recognized by an Act of the United States Congress, among many other honors. Burbank was brought up on a farm and received only an elementary education. His ability to perform experiments that produced plants with favorable characteristics depended more on his sense of intuition than on strict scientific methodology. A short synopsis of several of his books on plant improvement is available at http://www/discoveringbooks.com/burbank.

Jagadguru Paramahansa Yogananda in his international best seller *Autobiography of a Yogi* provides a detail account of Luther Burbank. The column "Agriculture and Horticulture Matters" was an instant hit in the newspapers and reflected Burbank's forgotten wisdom. Deep in his heart, the agriculturist desired people to read and follow Burbank's methods.

One of the engineers developed several zero-emission and closed cycle systems for several factories. He followed a "No-Effluent" and a "No-Smokestack" policy. The other engineer developed solar panels from natural materials to power homes. One physicist built swimming pools for all people in the city. The chemist, who was also a musician, opened schools to teach children sitar, violin, piano, tabla, etc.

The physicians helped people establish their own homoeopathic, Ayurvedic, allopathic, and eye clinics that performed both laser and cataract surgeries. Acupuncturists started offering micro acupuncture for people with degenerative eye diseases who had no other hope. The ayurvedic physicians started *panchakarma* (a program for the cleansing of the body, mind, and soul) clinics as well as ayurvedic clinics that were based on the ancient science of *shalakya tantra* to treat people with ear, nose, and eye related problems. Some public health officials even helped people start special centers that vaccinated children. As people started feeling more secure with the mortality rates of their children, women started having fewer and fewer children. A combination of both Eastern and Western forms of medicines were growing in healthy and complementary ways and seemed to help lower the overall costs of health care by offering diversity and choice.

As diverse systems of health care addressed the needs of the teeming population of Zindabad, an interesting success was unfolding in a remote rural area of Zindabad.

A small group of unemployed physicians and soil chemists were tired of facing a life of frustration and sub-optimal employment in the city of Zindabad. They relocated to a remote rural area that contained a variety of medicinal clays. Team members had read the classic book, *The Healing Power of Clay,* written by the French Naturopath Raymond Dextreit, first published in the 1950s. The intriguing book had compelled the team to read the growing body of international research on the healing uses of different types of clays, in particular, bentonite and pascalite. With additional information that they received from the International Pelotherapy Association (www.

pelotherapy.com), they launched a pelotherapy clinic alongside their western clinic in the remote rural area of Zindabad. The purpose of the clinic was to provide affordable health care to the rural poor who earned less than a dollar a day. Surprisingly, the team was making more money than most physicians in the city because they were able to export the excess of medicinal clay that could not be used in their clinics to spa operators located all over the world.

Ironically, the so-called friends of the physician team wrongly associated their business venture with filth and avoided their company. The local people on the other hand were oblivious to the politics of the city life; they simply enjoyed listening to the stories about pelotherapy in the clinic. For example, they knew how the Cro-Magnons and Cleopatra had a habit of bathing in clay and applying clay masks to stay beautiful and healthy. For a price that was worth a few pennies, the rural folk of Zindabad were enjoying facials, clay baths, and pelotherapy techniques that only the rich could afford in the Western countries.

Appreciative of the cyclical loop between soil and mankind, the rural folk slowly started developing a newfound respect for their ecology and environment. They discovered filtration and water storing mechanisms through the use of different clays. The rural folk returned organic matter back to the soil; they learned from the soil chemists not to eradicate pests completely, because this would also eliminate their natural predators. They began to see their soil as "living soil," containing billions of living organisms in every cubic centimeter. Through organic cultivation of their soil they discovered an increase in its carbon content and began to understand why organic farming could reduce global warming. The soil chemists were simply tapping into the innate and intuitive wisdom of the rural folk. The rural area of Zindabad was slowly transforming itself into a center that fostered agroecologists -- these people truly saw the connection between the soil, mankind, global warming, water, plant, and animal species.

On the contrary, people in the cities were subjecting their soil and water to more toxic hazards; the cost to treat waste-water kept increasing every year. The government passed on these higher costs as proportional increases in municipal taxes. Most people felt angry and hence avoided taxes through an established mechanism of corrupt practices. Therefore, the government was unable to collect all of its taxes. Consequently, fresh water supplied to homes was not adequately filtered because the government could not afford to make the additional investment required to provide safe drinking water. More and more companies were getting into the business of manufacturing portable water filtration products. The government wondered how it could change the culture of the city folk.

Some environmental groups recommended that Zindabad implement an eco based tax system as a pilot project. They wanted materials and services taxed based on the amount of toxic substances or the degree to which they ruined the environment. For major technical items such as TVs, Computers, VCRs, etc., the manufacturer refunded a portion of the eco-tax to the consumer when they turned in their used or non-functioning technical items. This tax rebate incentive encouraged a system of aggressive recycling and helped protect the environment and the water table.

The environmental groups wanted the system of income taxes replaced with eco-taxes. They reasoned that income taxes penalized work and hence in the longer term encouraged a variety of corrupt practices that were all harmful to the economy. On the contrary, eco-taxes, rightfully penalized things that people valued the least, such as the toxic content in products or the degree to which specific products ruined the eco-systems. Their powerful voices forced the central government to use Zindabad as a pilot for eco based taxes.

One of the biologists whose passion was animals started teaching people to have their own horse farms and dairy farms with cows and goats. With more decentralized milk production, people did not have to get up very early and stand in long milk lines. Slowly people took an interest in raising and keeping all kinds of exotic animals. Some entrepreneurs started their own petting zoos for children with deer, peacock, Australian kangaroo and others.

One of Professor Bhupati's students even became a myrmecologist, a person who studies ants. He was in great demand as a visiting lecturer at all the schools and colleges of Zindabad. He took several glass enclosures with different kinds of ants on his visits. He educated children on how ants harvested crops, raised insect as livestock, built roadways and bridges, how they did most of the turning and recycling of earth's materials and enriching the soil. He sometimes took his laptop and showed a program on the life of ants. His intention was to educate children on the contribution of ants to ecology as opposed to teaching the dry anatomical aspects of an ant. He sometimes quoted the world – renowned Harvard biologist and myrmecologist, E.O. Wilson, by saying, "It is the little things that run the world."

To the envy of his classmates, the myrmecologist also started a company to produce computer animated educational films on the life of ants and their contribution to ecology. When an unemployed biochemist approached him for ideas, the myrmecologist presented him with Erich Hoyt's book *The Earth Dwellers: Adventures in the Land of Ants.* He suggested the biochemist read the book and start a company that would breed ants. For ants also produced a natural antibiotic. The lowly Attini ants have been cultivating an effective antibiotic that has held off resistance for nearly 50 million years.[3] The myrmecologist was very sad when he related this fact to the biochemist because he knew that millions of years of evolutionary knowledge was disappearing every day all over the world due to the blind destruction of all tropical rainforests. He knew in his heart that nothing could replace this evolutionary knowledge since most human-developed antibiotics were slowly developing resistance.

To another unemployed biochemist he recommended growing a lot of flowering trees and setting up a bee farm. Most students wondered why biology was not taught as a science of living systems as opposed to a science of learning dry anatomical structures, After hearing the myrmecologist's lecture, the University students felt their training was quite "reductionist" and, therefore, had less appreciation on how living systems behaved. Their current education was lax in instructing how to establish a symbiotic relationship with nature.

This relationship would enable them to earn a decent living that was more aligned with the laws of nature.

Some highly entrepreneurial students of the University of Zindabad invented windmills that could be set up on the electric poles and they sold this power to the power plants. Other students established a joint venture with an American firm to supply power through solar balloon farms. Each solar balloon mimicked the technology of a magnifying glass and cost less than $2 to manufacture. Cool Earth Solar www. coolearthsolar.com had promised them that this technology was minimally disruptive and cost less than the traditional solar panels. A few other entrepreneurs teamed up with Calera www.calera.com in the United States to establish a carbon capture company. The company captured carbon from all chemical, coal, and power plants, and converted them into cement for building materials. Slowly a new breed of entrepreneurs mimicked this technology in vehicles that emitted emissions.

Most medical research coming out of the University of Zindabad was geared to preventive medicine. People noted that once a week fasting had an impact on cardiovascular disease and colorectal cancer. Just like a car, a human body also needed an engine tune up. The tradition of fasting was followed in ancient India but had been largely forgotten in modern times. Rearchers from America were closely following the methods of Panchakarma (five actions) clinics a cleansing and rejuvenating program for the body, mind, and soul. The researchers felt this had enormous potential for a preventive health franchise based model in America. In fact, a conglomerate, Green Business, Inc., was following a reverse model of compensation compared to many of its Western counterparts. The company attracted bright talent by increasing pension payouts and decreasing or minimizing to zero bonus or even stock options. The company believed that this encouraged early retirement and allowed people to follow community service early in their lives. Zindabad liked the model as it thought savings rate, unemployment rate, and total well being of an individual would actually improve in this manner.

Most economists of Zindabad noticed that a slow shift was beginning to happen, moving from blatant consumerism to an eco-economy where products were being naturalized. Creation of a new knowledge, a service, and a cultural economy was in slow bloom, much like the roses of Mr. & Mrs. Gulab Raja (the Rose King and the Rose Queen).

People were watching less television and connecting themselves more with nature. Tickets for movie sales were falling and people in Zindabad were now crowding Aravindra Bharathi, the arts and cultural centre of Zindabad. The economy of Zindabad now employed more people based on their unique preferences, tastes, and patterns. People found different kinds of professions closer to their homes, reducing travel time and commute costs by more than 20 percent. The creation of social capital was vastly enhanced.

But how many economists seriously care about the creation of social capital? Most models measure money and not social capital. Economic models do not capture the vibrancy of a community that tends to reveal itself like natural beauty.

The laymen intuitively understood the implication of social capital and its overall impact on the quality of living. They did not need an economic model for someone to prove that their life was better. They just desired for intellectualists to come down to their level. They were tired of listening to political debates on television between several political groups and sociologists. The sociologists debated that the economy was improving due to a critical mass created through leadership at the microscopic level by lay people. The politicians debated that the government and a macro-level, policy-oriented frame work was the reason for a change in the economy of Zindabad. Regardless of which group won the debate, the realization dawned on the common man that self-leadership, creativity, and enterprise were more important than dependence on the government.

Kakaji's students became adept at Yoga and started opening more Yoga schools. There was a sudden need for more swimming instructors. Students who returned from Russia started a school for gymnastics. The Zindabad sailing club reopened after having shut down for several years. The Asli Pani lake, which was now clear of toxic pollutants, had a sizable number of boats and yachts. Occupations in the fields of art, music, and culture emerged. *The very nature of diversity of the Zindabad landscape was expanding and transitioning from a consumer economy to a cultural economy.*

While all of this was going on, the journalists and the business graduates who had left Gulab consultants after its dissociation teamed together to start a new magazine, *The Urban Ecologist.* Scientists who used to publish scholarly journals began writing articles for the masses. Finally, their knowledge was conveyed in plain language to a wider variety of audience. The magazine provided unique and innovative ideas on the creation of arts, knowledge, and service enterprises.

The mission of the magazine was to naturalize all products and services so that they replenished nature instead of harming it. The mission was also to encourage and create a cultural economy. These two goals were totally interrelated at the magazine. The founding members clearly knew that one could not be created without the other. The magazine slowly became very popular, and its circulation expanded to other parts of the country through a decentralized approach. The entrepreneurs got permission to translate the magazine into almost 25 different local languages. Translation service as an industry became a booming business.

The magazine was published with recycled paper, and several farmers supplied paper pulp produced not from wood, but through waste plant materials such as bagasse, elephant grass, canary grass, Kenaf etc., The policy of the magazine was not to publish on paper produced from trees. The founders were concerned about the depletion of forests. This unique method of supply kept several local farmers employed.

As a consequence of all these changes, educational institutions developed new methods and models of teaching. People could specialize in a variety of different fields, even horse breeding. The growth of the knowledge, cultural, and service industry almost replaced the consumer product industry. There were some real tectonic shifts taking place in the economy. Every old-fashioned business model came under question. Economists noted that the quality of life seemed to be improving. Wealth was created at almost every level instead of within specific pockets. The degree in the growth of wealth on a per capita basis seemed uniform.

Gulab Rani also followed unique methods as a Government Minister. She was seldom available in her office. She traveled all over the country and held town hall meetings alongside local leaders. She preferred one-on-one conversations as opposed to memo writing or creating long-winded master plans. She realized through experience that written articles and reports were not conveying her ideas properly. Some of the State governments were simply replacing one bad practice with another. She wanted the principle of "eco-effectiveness" to be reality.

For example, some state governments thought that they could introduce more fuel-efficient cars to alleviate the problems of pollution. This was not Gulab Ranis' intentions; she wanted the government to strive for a mode of transportation that would actually nourish the atmosphere. Similarly, other states introduced stricter environmental regulations thinking that this was the right thing to do. Gulab Rani visited these states and showed them that these rules were simply stop-gap measures.

She urged the states to think of paradigm shifts in the human habits of manufacturing and consumption. She wanted companies to innovate their way out of regulations. She convinced several states that sustainable business practices were not cost additive; they were cost reducing. Sustainable business practices did not lower profits for a firm; they increased profits. Similarly, they did not decrease employment. On the contrary, they tended to uniformly increase employment.

When some Western-educated, industrial leaders challenged and criticized Gulab Rani, she did not bash their practices. She simply acknowledged their "eco-illiteracy." At times, she would freely present them books such as, *Cradle to Cradle: Remaking The Way We Make Things*, *Natural Capitalism: The Next Industrial Revolution*, *State of The World.* These books, written and published by Westerners, were recognized within their own countries as champions for the environment and as people who would change the way business would operate in the future. After presenting these books, she would urge them to read, expand their knowledge, and challenge her. Fortunately, most of her critics became her admirers rather than adversaries. Gulab Rani was neither a capitalist nor a communist; she was simply spreading the message of "eco-literacy." She believed in the triad of sustainable development: economy, equity, and ecology.

Gulab Rani never told businesses what to do; she never touched on peripheral parts. She wanted businesses to use their own creativity to come up with solutions. She did not want to diminish the diversity in the creative expression of thought. For example, when a business leader approached her and asked, "Is freon hurting the ozone layer. If yes, which compound should I use?" She answered the questions through a process of lecture and education.

Despite her attempts to educate people, she was constantly challenged. Once in a conference of business leaders, a major industrialist who manufactured and distributed pesticides through several sales representatives remarked: "Gulab Rani, your methods and approach mean death to my company, my employees, and my investors, We believe in growing the sales of our petrochemical-based pesticides. Now, you are basically asking me to close shop?"

Gulab Rani replied, "Sir. With all due respect, I am not trying to see the demise of your company. On the contrary, I am advocating how to transform your business or develop new business models. I am teaching and telling you how to survive. I will not be the cause of demise for your business. However, the competition will cause this demise. Business will sell intelligence and wisdom to the farmer on how to foil pests. Their focus will be on the plant, the land, the general health of the society, and environment. These businesses will train employees that will train farmers. They simply would not push a product. Now, don't you think this is a better business model that is more viable for the longer term? Is this not what you would want for your own company?"

She took a brief pause and continued, "When you align your employees to a greater good and craft a clear vision and a mission, I think your employees will derive more satisfaction from their work." The industrialist was puzzled and confused. "But, then, my investors and my employees care about how much pesticide is sold? How do I now transition to this business model? Do I grow a parallel model and see where I succeed? Will my employees feel more empowered with this new model?"

While most people in the crowd were still digesting these answers, a young hi-tech entrepreneur got up and asked a more blunt question to Gulab Rani, "Ms. Gulab Rani, are you for technology or are you against it?"

Gulab Rani responded, "I support technology that believes in upcycling; I do not support technology that believes in downcycling." Downcycling refers to reducing the quality of material over time. For example, when plastics are recycled, they get mixed with different other plastics to produce lower forms of plastic and finally one day you have very low quality plastic that it ends up scattered all over the landscape. However, in the case of upcycling the quality of these materials can improve over time or not degrade through constant recycling. So if your business model or your technology in combination with a people-supported or a government-supported recycling industry supports this concept and perpetuates the diversity of forests, the vitality of nature, rivers, oceans, air, soil, humans and animals, then, yes, I support your technology. I do not support technology that simply addresses raising our standard of living and is oblivious to all ecological issues."

In most cases, Gulab Rani answered the questions based on the temperament of the person asking the question. If someone were trained in the Western ways, she answered their questions by seeking the best knowledge from the West. If someone were trained in an Eastern way, she answered the question with an Eastern reference based on the little Vedic wisdom she had slowly acquired. For example, when she answered the young hi-tech entrepreneur she borrowed the terms Downcycling and Upcycling from the book

Cradle to Cradle: Remaking The Way We Make Things by the architect William McDonough and German chemist Michael Braungart. She intentionally chose the terms because she wanted people to read these kinds of books. The books harmonized the competing priorities of industrialists with the opinions of certain environmentalists with radical views. She knew that to implement change one has to show society several intermediate steps, options, and alternatives. She believed that radical opinions alienated people instead of engaging them.

The conference was about to end, but Gulab Rani could still sense a restlessness in the crowd. Kakaji, who was also at this conference, sensed this uneasiness. He calmed himself and with a steady and a clear voice said, "Time for one last question." An anxious entrepreneur of computer-related parts and equipment got up, looked straight into Kakaji's eyes and said. "I am confused with Gulab Rani's response. She sounds philosophical. Kakaji, can you tell me whether computers are good or bad for the environment?"

Kakaji responded, "We are not here in this conference to denounce or criticize a product, or an industry, or a service. We are here to focus on the human being. The human being is the cause and the creator of all problems. Every product, company, or a system has a purpose to serve. It is up to the human being to use the product for the right purpose. If you used the computer to surf the Internet to creatively address the cleaning up of the Ganges river, you did the right thing. However, if you were finished with the effective life of the computer and threw this computer into the Ganges river – a bundle of cadmium, lead, arsenic, mercury, and several other innumerable toxic materials… you simply committed an act of crime and genocide on all ecosystems."

Kakaji paused and then continued, "What Gulab Rani was trying to tell you is to naturalize the components in your computer so that everything biodegrades back into nature. We miniaturized computers, a step in the right direction. Now, we need to make the components more biodegradable one at a time so that waste becomes food. The impossible has always been made possible. Gulab Rani was taking the long-term view, and I am trying to give you the short-term view. Both views are equally important for your own personal and professional growth. Therefore, sir, this conference is about presenting you with opportunities to expand your wisdom." The conference ended with smiles on most faces. Gulab Rani and Kakaji knew they had made some difference in the way people would begin to think.

Gulab Rani's association with Kakaji helped her build a mental bridge that integrated the best wisdom of the East and of the West. She believed good wisdom emanated from all countries of the world. No matter how much she learned, she knew in her heart that the secret for infinite wisdom was in training the body, the mind, and the soul. She believed that countries and people mostly collaborated in the wrong areas for their solutions. Regardless of education, people and businesses were more susceptible to superficiality and the immediacy of television and social media.

Gulab Rani knew the mental dilemmas that faced most people. She found it helpful sometimes to mention the Gaia Theory of James Lovelock and Lynn Margulis.[4] Gaia is the mythical name for Mother Earth. It lends its name to scientific theory; it portrays earth as a royal super- organism, where each animal and plant serves a specific function that helps to maintain a stable, living environment. Such a broad approach allows dispassionate analysis of the effects of pollution and toxic waste, the greenhouse effect, acid rain, and the murder of marine life. The Gaian approach also provides a way to distinguish those ecological problems that are real and urgent and those that are either unreal or real but less significant. Several books available on this subject, including one non-technical primer on Gaia for lay people, called *The Guide to Gaia* by Michael Allaby.

Gulab Rani directed people to the Web, a book, or a theory that would help answer their questions. Once, she told a businessman about a process called, "The Natural Step" pioneered by Dr. Karl-Henrik Robert, one of Sweden's leading cancer researchers.[5] The Natural Step process was endorsed by Swedish royalty and leaders in science and business. Schools and households are familiar with the process. Its principles are active in such areas as municipal water systems, furniture manufacture, and "clean agriculture" practices In brief, "The Natural Step" process states that prosperity and life itself depend on whether matter is concentrated and structured, or whether it is dispersed and mixed, that is, chaos. If matter on earth is systematically concentrated and structured into ordered matter, that is the fundamental principle of prosperity and health. If we disperse it and consume its quality into chaos, that is the basis of death and poverty.

The laws of thermodynamics, which we have known since the 19th century, state that it is impossible to maintain quality in any closed system if it is completely closed. Any completely closed system is doomed. The end stage is complete chaos of matter.

This chaos is prevented by energy coming in from outside the system. In the case of Earth, the sun provides that energy. The sun energizes green cells, systematically concentrating and structuring matter into net quality. All other attempts to produce – as in our cells, for instance, dissolve more fuel (in this case food) into dispersed waste than the growth of the body in itself represents. It is the same for car manufacturing, and other processes that are not fueled directly or indirectly by the sun.

To maintain prosperity and health, we must not dissolve more matter into dispersed waste than is reconstituted back into the ordered forms again. Gulab Rani explained to her colleagues that this is the overall cyclic principle of the whole biosphere where we live. She explained to those who would listen that if you draw a flow diagram (which "The Natural Step" has done, together with physicists and a group of other scientists), you can see four overall principles, which, according to Karl-Henrik Robert, are "non-negotiable and absolute." The beauty of this model is that since it is absolute, you can audit yourself in that direction. The author outlined these "Four System Conditions" as follows:

1.Substances from the earth's crust must not systematically increase in nature.

Fossil fuels, metals, and other materials must not be extracted at a faster pace than their slow redeposit into the earth's crust. Otherwise, quality will be lost due to the inevitable spread of waste and their accumulation beyond which irreversible changes occur. Today, in practical terms, this means radically reduced mining and use of fossil fuels.

2.Substances produced by society must not systematically increase in nature.

Substances must not be produced at a faster pace than they can be broken down and integrated into the cycles of nature or deposited into the earth's crust. Otherwise, quality will be lost due to the inevitable spread of substances and their accumulation towards often unknown limits, beyond which irreversible changes occur. In practical terms, this means decreased production of natural substances that are accumulating, and a phase-out of all persistent and unnatural substances, such as plastic, freon, or PCBs.

3. The physical basis for the productivity and diversity of nature must not be systematically diminished.

The ecosystem must not be harvested or manipulated in such a way that productive capacity and diversity systematically diminish. Our health and prosperity depend on the capacity of nature to reconcentrate and restructure wastes into resources. Today, this means sweeping changes in our use of natural resources for agriculture, forestry, fishing, and planning societies.

4.Energy and other resources must be used wisely and efficiently.

Basic human needs must be met with the most resource-efficient methods possible, including a just resource distribution. Humanity must prosper with a resource metabolism meeting the above three system conditions. This is necessary for social stability and cooperation in making future change. Today, in practical terms, this means an increased technical and organizational efficiency in the world, including a more resource-economical lifestyle.

Gulab Rani knew that in order to satisfy the above four conditions, an equitable cultural economy was more suitable for the country. Intuitively, she blended the scientific understanding that she gained from her training with the Vedic wisdom she gathered through her association with Kakaji. She knew that Mahatma Gandhi stood for such principles. However, he lived in an age when his principles could not be communicated in a manner that was most beneficial for the current state of the society. The negative impact of pollution, waste, and technology was not fully manifested during the time of Gandhi.

The success of Gulab Rani and her team inspired journalists to write articles describing the transformation of Zindabad. This was the only city in India with a zero percent increase in the growth of population without any investment in population programs. The reversal of ecological phenomena and the transformation to a cultural-, knowledge-, and a service-based economy had given the people a sense of accomplishment, security, and well-being. People could again enjoy their rose gardens.

When *The Urban Ecologist* launched its first issue, the publication sponsored a poetry contest on the environmental state of India 65 years after its independence. I submitted the following poem:

Sixty–Five Years of Environmental Independence

Squander we did all our groundwater,

Dig we did millions of tube wells in over fifty-five years

We fractured our skin and dehydrated our bodies,

We deprived our poor plants of oxygen,

We kept building dams that displaced villagers,

... and, then built reservoirs that submerged forests

And farmland.

We keep accelerating urbanization through displacement.

We keep pouring asphalt and building more roads,

We address the increasing need for a car and the decreasing

Need for a bicycle,

We choke our roads with diesel-guzzling vehicles,

Our road traffic contributing to 70 percent of our urban

Air pollution[6]

We then wonder why God caused all those premature

Deaths!

With minimally existent pollution control policies, laws,

Or equipment,

We generate over 50 million tons of solid waste each year.[7]

Not knowing what needs done,

We dump our oceans and landfills with solid waste and

Leaky contaminants.

DDT or Atrazan, we care not for life,

Ironically, we gave a Nobel prize to the person who

Discovered the insecticidal property of DDT

Through contaminated water,

We create terrible communicable diseases.

We then wonder why God has no care!

In states like Tamil Nadu we reduced our evergreen forests

To less than 1 percent of its original area.[8]

We then wonder on climate change and lack of rain

Water.

We stress our soil, we stress our water,

We stress our forests, we stress our livestock,

We stress our environment, we stress our nature,

We stress ourselves and decrease all output.

But yet in a mistaken glee we think we increase output.

We accelerate in all areas we want to decelerate,

We decelerate in all areas we want to accelerate,

We ignore the obvious and address the obscure.

11

Establishing a Framework for Creating a Cultural Economy

While coming close to the end of this poetic story, one could ponder, "Sustainable living is fine; but where are the employment opportunities and how do we create them?" The question is justified.

I attempted to provide answers in the previous chapters through poetry, storytelling interwoven with non-fictional material, and reference to resources to help shape personal, entrepreneurial, and professional decisions. The focus of this chapter is an attempt to create a cultural economy of sustainable living with the triad of sustainable development: economy, equity, and ecology.

What may ultimately be right for the country is fostering a system where diversity is a strength and not a liability. When we start looking at every man, woman, and child regardless of race, color, caste, or creed, we can create a system where power lies with everyone. When we start taking power away from people, we develop imperfections in a system. Similarly, when power is with people, they need to understand the law of reciprocity with nature. A mixed system of both formal and informal education needs to encourage such a vision. Bear in mind that I am not referring to any kind of a system here.

We have confused our education system with all kinds of labels and politico-economic systems. Even Adam Smith in the 1700s spoke of systems with small traders and buyers. We came up with the labels and confused our youth. We now have to embark on a process of deconditioning our minds. Let people explore what is right within the framework of broad theories and the unchangeable laws of nature.

It is important here to clarify the distinction between a theory that is eternal in nature and that which is a man-made theory. For example, capitalism is a man-made theory; so is communism. Man-made theories have both pros and cons. Therefore, simply for the sake of convenience, we want to readily adopt the pros of a man-made theory without addressing the cons. This is where humanity tends to make its mistakes. For example, we want to adopt hi-tech technology, but we don't want to address recycling. It is primarily for this reason that I suggest the importance of informal education in India along with formal education. We need both, a hybrid of the two.

Eternal theories, on the other hand, are truth. Adoption of the theory produces the outcome as it was predicted or the theory just states the fact. A democratic society needs to seek opportunity based on truth. People need choices, and they need to assess what works and what does not based on their own inherent, unique, God-given traits. The greatest sages of India, Gandhi, Tagore, and others were specialists in both formal and informal education. People in America are also transitioning from traditional formal specialties to informal specialties. Society keeps giving these people new labels, including New-Age gurus, Environmentalists, Ecologists, Ecospiritualists and Thought Leaders.

No one will refute gravity or the revolution of the earth around the sun. Both concepts are eternal truths. Similarly, no one will refute the law of reciprocity, the law of symbiosis in the ecological kingdom, or other such eternal truths. We focus so much of our energy teaching problem-solving that we lose sight of the eternal truth. We would rather spend a lifetime understanding why a leaf on a tree has a different color from some other tree than understanding the usefulness of the tree itself. This does not mean such a scientific pursuit is bad. It just means that our energy and focus on the acquisition of knowledge is distorted. Once the broad theories or the eternal truths come into focus, people will find their own solutions within those theories. The results can only be wholesome and conducive for our overall well-being as opposed to life being a constant struggle of years spent specializing in our own areas of interest, making us oblivious to how our interests impact others and our world. We just want the benefits of the issue at hand, and do not want to address the drawbacks – let it be someone else's problem. Since reaching perfection is not an overnight phenomenon, we need to focus on practical solutions that will lead us closer to the goal.

Development centered at the grassroots level is an appropriate approach for policy. Development imposed through external sources can sometimes be disruptive to human relationships and the general way of living. When people can exercise the ability to gain control and use resources effectively, they become more creative and empowered. A grand vision must encourage people to become more close to natural processes rather than being alienated from them. We need people-centered technologies, processes that encourage reciprocity, and processes that value ecology, ecosystems, and nature. Everything that we do must mimic the natural order that life itself has created and teaches to us on a constant basis. All of this knowledge already exists. What is lacking is man's will and the creative force to help shift us from a consumer economy to a cultural economy.

As an opinion:

A cultural economy increases ecosystem diversity,

A consumer economy without regard for nature can

Diminish ecosystem diversity,

Thus:

A cultural economy maximizes diversity in a simplified

Economic system,

A consumer economy maximizes diversity in a more complex

Economic system.

Thus:

*A cultural economy radiates power outward and maximizes equity
in wealth,*

A consumer economy radiates power inward and minimizes

Equity in wealth

Thus:

A cultural economy supports an educational system that

Trains the body, the mind, and the soul,

A consumer economy rewards an educational system that

Trains the mind.

Thus:

A cultural economy maximizes the attention on the soul

And minimizes attention on the sense,

A consumer economy maximizes the attention on the sense

And minimizes attention on the soul

Thus:

A cultural economy addresses overall preventive health,

A consumer economy creates institutions to address

Preventive health.

Thus:

A cultural economy may minimize the impact of all

Living costs,

A consumer economy may maximize the impact of al living

Costs.

Thus:

A cultural economy accelerates the creation of social capital

And replenishes natural capital,

A consumer economy accelerates the creation of monetary

Capital and depletes natural capita.

It is important to bear in mind that the reference here to a consumer economy is one where the economy has little regard for nature. The current general state of most institutions is to deplete nature. I am not an authority on the issues mentioned in this book. I am not even qualified to provide an agenda. I only reflect feelings as a free person, and I hope many share this view.

Within India we have pockets of consumer economy and few pockets of cultural economy. Historically, we had a cultural economy. The reference here to a cultural economy is broad. It encompasses all new forms and systems of formal and informal or non-formal education, embraces an eco-friendly economy, establishes connectivity of human life to natural life, and fosters an environment where people are enamored with the giver of earthly gifts. The springboard for sustainable living is a cultural economy. One cannot establish a sustainable economy without creating a cultural economy, and without addressing the underlying dynamics of the system of education. While these include formal, informal, and place-based theories, the system of education also places equal emphasis on the development of the body, the mind, and the soul. Our current system of education places emphasis on only on filling our mind; we have become alienated from our heritage and our earth.

The complicated structural dynamics and our rich and deep culture automatically beckon us to start a cultural economy. Instead of listening and focusing on our natural strengths, we have resorted to an erroneous focus on linear growth at the expense of nature. This may increase the long-term costs of the country. Each one of us has to undertake an introspective analysis to verify whether this hypothesis is true or not. One example is to compare India in the pre-mid 60s to the post-mid 60s. The population of India more than tripled in the last 40 years. Yet, our approach is still "top-down" and not bottom-up."

Most people want reason, logic, and a sequential thinking approach on any process. The whole-system thinking is complex because it sees patterns, and it analyzes the objective and the subjective. What we need for the future is a redefinition of the word "Progress" Most economists do not bring the depletion of nature into their equation on measuring progress. However, some eminent economists want to change the way we define "progress" or even to replace simple definitions like GNP with GPI or the Genuine Progress Indicator. The GPI is a comprehensive measure of well-being that incorporates environmental and social factors.

The verse below helps define "Progress" in a cultural economy:

Progress means not declaring war with nature

... it means making peace with nature.

Progress means not exploring outer worlds

... it means exploring inner worlds.

Progress means not the satisfaction of the sense

... it means satisfaction of the soul.

Progress means not sharing and caring

...it means sharing and caring.

Progress means not all technological wonder

... it means natural wonder that embraces holistic

Technology.

Progress means not all scientific excellence

... it means science that blends with nature.

Progress means not ecology that adapts to technology

... it means technology that adapts to ecology.

Progress means not a few powerful people

... it means many powerful people in many diversified areas.

Progress means not just an emphasis on the Yang

... it means a holistic emphasis on the Yin and the Yang.

Finally, progress is simultaneously addressing all the above. The lack of diversity in the current definition of the word "Progress" has caused much confusion. It appears that humanity is set to follow only one path: the accumulation of wealth without regard for nature. Unless there is a clear understanding of the word "Progress," there is bound to be much confusion among several different groups of people. Environmentalists and ecologists think that growth is destroying the world, and businesses think environmentalists are holding people back from becoming more progressive. These arguments are generally confusing because of the varying degrees of knowledge on eco-literacy and systems concepts among the several groups.

Therefore, the answer lies in creating, fostering, and growing a healthy culture – a culture where good health thrives over sickness, where equity in prosperity thrives over poverty, where everything is a nutrient (zero waste). A healthy culture is a culture where man mimics the laws of nature to the best to of his abilities. In business, it is a culture where linear thinking processes in manufacturing and/or creation of organizational systems are replaced by cyclical thinking processes. Let us be extremely clear: we need to foster and create a culture and not a system such as capitalism or communism or socialism. The approach here is not whether one belongs to the left or right. The approach should be one where the individual creativity of all individuals dovetails into a grand vision that has unequivocal respect for the simple laws of nature.

Many global non-profit organizations are founded on principles that touch on such a grand vision. The goal of most of these organizations is exactly the same—a deep respect for natural life. Phrases like environmental movement, green movement, eco-movement, sustainable movement, holistic technology, green technology, and no-waste economy, all in one way or another, tend to connote either a sustainable economy or a close respect to nature. But all these things in my opinion, are only possible with the creation of a cultural economy. Therefore, whether one believes in the philosophy of non-profit organization or a specific religion, the principles of ecology and the respect for nature are similar. For example, the Vedic seers regarded the earth as "sacred space" for the consecrated endeavors and aspirations of humankind and for the practice of restraint and responsibility. In their use of earth's resource, Jains take their cue from "the bee that sucks honey in the blossoms of a tree without hurting the blossom and strengthening itself." Indeed, the Jain faith declares unequivocally that waste and creating pollution are acts of violence.

According to H.E Laxmi Mall Singhvi, President of the World Congress on Human Rights and President Emeritus of the Authors' Guild of India, "The spiritual, ethical, individual and collective dimensions of human life constitute a continuum, encompassing the whole of the Indic heritage and transcending all segments and fragments. The Vedic, Upanishadic, Jain and Buddhist traditions perceived this and together built an enduring spiritual, intellectual and cultural foundation for an environment-friendly value system and a balanced lifestyle."[1]

It is time we created cultural diversity, sustainable living, and a cultural economy that measures progress of any entity on how it interacts with all other entities, We need to develop a total systems concept that fosters such a culture. Unfortunately, in the present climate, we focus too much attention on the peripheral parts, do enormous amounts of research on the parts, and produce tons of information on questions that have little relevance or value. The critics, if all this was right, ask: "Has it made any impact in our day-to-day lives? As long as we keep destroying our ecological and social structure in the name of "progress," we are simply adding unnecessary layers of costs and deteriorating quality of life in the society not only for ourselves but also for all living species around us and generations to come. Yes it does increase GNP, but it is irrelevant and meaningless.

Most of our research and innovations are incremental improvements in linear –based production systems, and we are not thinking in terms of creating cyclical systems. Cyclical systems are evolving, adjusting, non-competing, and cooperative. They create products that are metabolized back into nature; In fact, nature itself grew not by domination, competition, and control. It grew by participation, cooperation, and symbiosis. When a human being ingests food, his system metabolizes that food. Similarly, when a cosmic body, "Mother Earth", ingests a product, it needs to metabolize the same. While there is some thought on creating cyclical production systems, and materials and products that are either metabolized or absorbed back into nature, less emphasis is being paced on developing cyclical systems as it relates to the provisions of major services such as in education, government, planning, banking, and lending. For this reason, a cultural economy needs fostering.

For example, in a cultural economy, if a child goes to sleep very late in the night on a regular basis; an informal school will classify the child as being "not-progressive." This is because the child will eventually increase the costs of health care and be a burden on society. Benjamin Franklin said, "Early to bed, early to rise, makes a body healthy, wealthy, and wise." There are numerous studies in obeying the circadian rhythms of the body. Again, such eternal truths are innumerable. Once we develop a system to learn and live within their constraints, we will see marked improvements in terms of lowering the costs in all areas of our lives. The solution is simple, cyclical, and systems-oriented.

Like every other common man, we see what is happening on a day-to-day basis. We read the thoughts of so many people who are generally concerned with our ecosystems either in the newspaper, magazine, book or online. Perhaps we even write about these events. Often, the written words stir our hearts and minds. These electrifying thoughts help align all our molecules in a manner that is consistent with the thought process of the writers. It is through their wisdom, that we within our own defined identity draw our opinions and conclusions. This in essence, is the wonder of nature called diversity.

The common man, like us, typically recycles thoughts of either saintly personalities, eco-spiritualists, or other inspired personalities wanting to do good for the world. If we watch their actions carefully, they never provide canned solutions. They give guidance, direction, and inspiration. They want people to develop their own solutions. People and countries have to do the sifting between what is right and what is wrong. This is a constant process and not a finite, linear one. Therefore, the government must only facilitate the framework. Their only job is to communicate a very clear vision, and let the people work the things out. They should not assume a role to force these decisions; otherwise, power will then start flowing inward.

The government can facilitate the process by scrapping the current system of income taxes and slowly transition to a method where products and components that ruin nature are taxed. In countries like India and China it is urban air pollution that is a major cause of disease and also climate change. Let us then creatively tackle these problems first. Let us utilize the 80/20 rule, where 20 percent of the products that cause 80 percent of the problems are taxed first. All of these actions will encourage eco-friendly entrepreneurship. Such entrepreneurship may create more opportunities for employment rather than fewer opportunities. If we simply tamed the technology that we already have for the good of ecology, environment, and humankind, we would realize that the opportunities are much more immense. Let us use and transform existing technology to create "ecological health" as opposed to "ecological mess." Such paradigm shifts will also meet the criteria of more equity, healthier ecology, and a healthier economy in the community.

It is my theory, like several other people, that several nations are endowed with diversity, and we need to protect this diversity in all its facets because I consider the protection and fostering of diversity itself as an eternal truth. It allows us to be less judgmental of things. Such qualities can only strengthen us and not weaken us. When forests are diverse, there is strength in the forests; when people eat fruits of different color and variety, they become healthier; when corporations hold brainstorming sessions, they want a diverse group.

In any aspect of life, diversity adds value. According to Fritjof Capra, "Diversity is a strategic advantage to a community if, and only if, there is a vibrant network of relationships, if there is a free flow of information through all the links of the network. Then diversity is a tremendous strategic advantage. However, if there is fragmentation, if there are subgroups in the network or individuals who are not really part of the network, then diversity can generate prejudice, it can generate friction, and can generate violence."[2]

He further adds, "If different kinds of people make different kinds of mistakes, and if information about different kinds of mistakes is shared and travels through the network, then very quickly the community will figure out the smartest ways to solve certain problems or smartest ways to adapt to changes."[3]

Therefore, diversity is strength as long as we have a vibrant network of relationships, and cyclical flows of energy and information. When we restrict these flows, we create suspicion and distrusts, and diversity becomes a hindrance.

The poem below amplifies my thoughts on how we can foster a cyclical flow of energy and information that will foster diversity:

India endowed with 27 major languages,

More than 300 dialects,

What a booming business we have as a "Translation

Industry"

Endowed with a multitude of cultures,

Malayalam, Telugu, Tamil, Kannada, Hind, Punjabi,

Sindhi, Urdu, English, etc.,

What a booming business we have in food, textiles, and

Millions of consumables.

Endowed with a multitude of rivers and lakes,

Ganges, Yamuna, or even the small Hussain Sagar Lake,

What a booming business we have in protecting these rivers

And in sporting events.

Endowed with a multitude of health philosophies,

Ayurveda, Homoeopathy , Allopathy,. Tao, Reiki, Tachyon,

And the like.

What a booming business we have as a health industry.

Endowed with millions of worship places,

Temples, Churches, Masjids, Synagogues and the like,

What a booming non-profit business we have in religion.

Endowed with millions of species of trees and animals,

Deciduous, Conifers, and other innumerable

Categorizations.

What a booming business we have in not destroying but

Simply breeding them.

Endowed with thousands of educational philosophies,

Formal, Non-Formal, Vocationnel, Religious, Spiritual, etc.,

What a booming business we have as an Education

Industry.

Endowed with best ideas from everywhere on the globe,

East, West, North, or South,

What a booming business we have in creating an

Information Enterprise Industry.

Endowed with the best minds on Sustainable Thinking,

The grass-roots movement or the Eco-Movements,

What a booming business we have in establishing the best

Sustainable Technologies.

We do have the best diversity in the world. Let us protect every ounce and inch of this diversity. This is our strength and not our weakness.

Let us not diminish this diversity but rather let us help increase this diversity. The very nature of nature itself is diversity; it abhors uniformity. Let us open the windows of our minds and the hearts of our souls.

Certainly, I am not indicating that any of the experiments in this book are correct. I present them to help start a debate. It is for individuals to assess for themselves what course is right or wrong. What we are oblivious to in this world is the obvious connections between health care costs, living costs, and the mechanistic view of the technological progress of this world. We are acting on a geological and biological order of magnitude. We are changing the chemistry of the planet.

Think of any product that you touch, feel, and use; is it metabolized or absorbed back into the earth? We are altering the great hydrological cycles. We are weakening the ozone layer, saturating the air, the water, the ocean, the fish, the fruits, the vegetables, and the soil with toxic substances so that we can never bring them back to their original state of purity. That the changes taking place are of this order and magnitude can be supported by reference to a conference held in September 1986 in Washington DC on the future of living species sponsored by the National Academy of Sciences and the Smithsonian Institution. Our foremost biologists expressed forebodings concerning the future. Each of their statements shows the immense correlation between the environment and health.

At the conference, E.O. Wilson from Harvard indicated that we are losing 10,000 species each year and that this rate of loss is increasing. Norman Myers, a specialist in the rainforests and vegetation of the world, said that the "impending extinction spasm" is likely to produce the 'greatest single setback to life's abundance and diversity since the first flickering of life almost four billion years ago.'[4] Other speakers agreed that our present extinction of living forms is, in its order of magnitude, paralleled only by the great geological and climatic upheavals that changed the earth in the distant past.

In the words of Thomas Berry, a historian of cultures:

"The natural world is the maternal source of our being as earthlings and the life-giving nourishment if our physical, emotional, aesthetic, moral, and religious existence. The natural world is the larger sacred community to which we belong. To be alienated from this community is to become destitute in all that makes us human. To change this community is to diminish our own existence."[5]

Therefore, we can conclude that continued technological progress without regard to nature diminishes our very own existence; the imbalance is reflected as rising costs in all areas of living.

No matter how grand a vision one has, it is unreasonable to think things will change overnight. But we have to begin somewhere through small-scale, bottoms-up experiments, small-scale alliances, creative partnerships among several institutions, and most important, individuals who are willing to give things a try. Testing opposing ideas may only broaden our vision. Small-scale experiments will not stifle free markets. They can certainly pose a healthy challenge to existing business models. They allow us opportunities to learn what may work and what may not.

The thoughts and ideas in this book may or may not be correct. We all live in a free society and let individuals have their own opinions. I am no expert; I am a lay person who wants his opinion heard. I believe there is no denying the fact that principles that support life need to be our focus; if we truly want to contain costs and improve quality in all areas and all facets of our life. Above all, living in a sustainable manner may just nourish our souls, and the key to living in a sustainable manner is the restoration of a deep and a rich culture.

The sages and the great saints knew this truth. Therefore, they worked at the very deepest level – the human and his consciousness. They asked us not only to identify our own divinity but also to see the same divinity in all beings. Addressing this, we would have automatically addressed everything else. Therefore, our greatest saints are the wisest guardians of the earth ship and all beings on this ship. If we are losing 10,000 species each year, we cannot deny the truth that in some way it is affecting our own lives as well.

I end this book with the quote that I discovered on the website of the Sustainability Institute.[6]

"Can we move nations and people in the direction of sustainability? Such a move would be a modification of society comparable in scale to only two other changes: the Agricultural Revolution of the late Neolithic and the Industrial Revolution of the past two centuries. These revolutions were gradual, spontaneous, and largely unconscious. This one will have to be a fully conscious operation, guided by the best foresight that science can provide. If we actually do it, the undertaking will be absolutely unique in humanity's stay on earth."

---- William D. Ruckleshaus

Afterword

On July 2, 2002, my father, Dr. L. Venkataratnam, a well known and a highly respected Horticulturist and Environmentalist both in Hyderabad and in India, died in a road accident. His car swerved off the road in Sangareddy, Hyderabad, and hit a banyan (peepul) tree. He died instantaneously while asleep on the passenger side of the car. Well wishers of the family offered a philosophic interpretation; they felt that the trees that he loved and cared for simply fulfilled his desire for a painless death. His life was taken away by a tree that is considered highly sacred in India. While this philosophic interpretation was comforting, it certainly did not excuse the crude road construction of India.

His death was primarily due to bad road construction. Some of the roads in Hyderabad have a one-foot vertical drop at their edges. If one is on the edge of the road, one can simply lose control of the car since driving on a road is akin to driving on a bridge in some places in Hyderabad. Tragic as it was, the very ideals that my father stood for took away his life. He was one of the founding members in Hyderabad for the Society for the Preservation of Environment and Quality of Life (SPEQL).

This society had also started a magazine called *Hyderabad Bachao* (Save Hyderabad). His life was marked with a missionary zeal and a relentless pursuit for the growth of trees in Hyderabad and for the preservation of environment and quality of life. Ironically, he died for the very ideals he worked for all his life. Perhaps his tragic death is a reminder to a new generation on the ideals of his work and mission.

While my father never read this book or gave his seal of approval on the contents I know very well in my heart that his life inspired the very essence of this book. At the time of his death at 83, he was enrolled in a computer class. He was proud to be the oldest in the class. He challenged his grandchildren that he would teach them e-mail, Internet, and the preparation of Power Point presentations, In the evenings he sometimes attended the Ramakrishna Mission. In his later life, he was enamored with their teachings.

My father sometimes reminded me of the great Luther Burbank. Like Burbank, my father had developed and improved the armamentarium of plant life with his inventions such as the Ratnam Shahi grape, the seedless custard apple, seedless tomatoes, seedless mangoes, etc. Because of his efforts, Rama Koteswar Rao and later Somaraju, progressive grape growers in Hyderabad received the prestigious "Padma Shri" Award for recording 100 tons of Anabeshahi grape per hectare. This was considered an All India record. He published over 200 publications and authored four books. However, not once in his lifetime did he speak or trumpet his accomplishments. He kept up with the times. He was highly ambitious, yet not a materialist. He admitted the child of his housekeeper in an elementary school by paying the necessary capitation fee because he believed that the poor man's child needed the same quality of education as was afforded to his own children. He worked tirelessly with the enthusiasm of a teenager as Chairman of the non-profit, Agri-Horticultural Society of Hyderabad. Under his tutelage, this institution grew to generate several lakhs of rupees. He was least interested in name and fame. He simply worked because it was the right thing to do.

His belief system was firmly grounded in the East, yet, his temperament and action was that of a Western man. If someone had asked me, "Show me one man and woman who represent the ideals of this book?" it certainly would be my father and my mother. I am certain there are many more individuals such as them that I may not have come across them in person. My mother was the backbone for my father. My father was symbolic for the creation of a cultural economy, and my mother, to this day, exemplifies the finest qualities in sustainable living. The essence of this book is a eulogy of their life. I never knew why I chose to write this book. However, the message became intuitively clear with my father's demise.

I urge every reader to find such examples or emulate the life and work of such personalities. This book is mainly a reflection of the life that was led by my father and a life that is continued to be led by my mother. Subconsciously, they infused into their daily actions the wisdom of the East with the practicality and efficiency of the West.

We are in state of confusion today because we are not harnessing the power of centuries of cultural and ecological wisdom. We give more importance to rituals rather than following the spirit behind the rituals. We plagiarize the West without infusing wisdom and common sense in out plagiarism. The simple aspect of the crude road construction that took my father's life demonstrates this. Until and unless we infuse more wisdom and common sense in our day-to-day actions, reconnect ourselves with our ancient teachings, correctly question our mode of existence in an overall ecological context, and show greater sincerity in our everyday intentions, then, and only then, may it be possible to pursue the ideals in this book. The crux of the issue lies in the order by which the world operates. We first build economies, then address ecology, then address sustainability, and then finally culture. It should be the opposite way. How beautiful the world would be if every individual and institution shifted to this paradigm.

For one last time, simply share my fantasy:

First Steps to Building a Cultural Economy

Let human culture influence a technological culture,

Let not technological culture influence a human culture.

Wisdom, spirituality, or Vedic thought can all foster a

Human culture,

Let one maximize what the heart likes and minimize what

The sense likes.

Through a glorious human culture we can build a sound

Ecological culture.

In ecology lie embedded the secrets of true technology,

In technology may not lie embedded the secrets of attaining

True ecology.

Am I philosophizing? Let me embellish then through a

Simple example:

In ecology was embedded multicolored cotton bolls,

But, then, man made extinct the colored cotton bolls,

Multiplied he did the white cotton bolls and dyed them

With toxic chemicals.

Through technology he then sought to eradicate the problem

He created in ecology,

Little did he realize that embedded in ecology were all the

Answers for technology.

The puzzle lies juxtaposed not in our minds but in our

Hearts,

Let us trap our minds and untrap our hearts.

What sometimes appears primitive is ecologically

Sophisticated,

What sometimes appears sophisticated is ecologically

Primitive.

Am I philosophizing? Let me embellish then through another

Example:

Compare then the house that is built with concrete, steel,

And a plethora of inorganic chemicals,

With a house that used all organic and indigenously

Developed materials.,

The last of such houses vanished with great cultures and

Civilizations,

The modern inorganic house attracted many a worker from

Rural to the urban centers,

The organic house retained the worker in the rural town and

Centers.

We encourage systems of education that create forward flows

In labor from rural to the urban,

When all along we needed to create backward flows in

Labor from urban to the rural.

For we foster a system of education that creates an army of

"problem solvers".

When all along we needed to create a system of education

That created "problem preventers".

A strong culture can create "problem preventers' and an

Economy can create "problem solvers".

We may need both, but not always grand solutions in

Creating problems and solving problems

Let us question the real source of our mistakes and not

Perpetuate the same.

Through lopsided strategies we intend to shape our minds for

Technological sophistication,

But how often do we perfect technology and systems for

Ecological sophistication,

We continue on with ever-increasing justification and

Pontification

... only to get lost in superficial charm and mesmerization.

Let's not forget, Respect for all life is still the foundation.

Was even confirmed by the Native American in his, "Great Law of Peace."

Culture, Culture, Culture ... still the very basis of our sustenance.

In the short term, people need to discard the notion that it is the government's job to create an economic plan. Instead, they should listen to the profound words of Mother Teresa: "Do not wait for leaders; do it alone, person-to-person." The government, after all, is only a collective expression of the will of the people. Once there is greater will and consciousness in society, the government will likely consider replacing income taxes with eco-taxes. Educational institutions will restructure their strategies to create programs that encourage holistic growth in the individual, where he uses all his faculties of the mind, the body, and the soul to develop technologies and businesses that are aligned with nature. The solution lies in questioning, refining, and improving daily interactions with the entire ecological environment.

Small shifts from a petrochemical and a toxic technological era to a technological era aligned with the environment have already emerged in various ecological movements around the world, Countries that willingly embrace such a holistic perception either through the development of a strong culture, practices of sustainability and spirituality will succeed in creating prosperity for all citizens. A cultural and sustainable economy can only be born by addressing the basic and the obvious, not the obscure and the complex. The richness of any economy lies in its basic respect for all forms of life, living or nonliving.

Footnotes

Introduction

1.Ackerman, D., Deep Play, Random House, New York, NY. 1999. P. 130

Chapter 2

1.Agarwal A., Economic globalization must be followed by ecological globalization" In an interview with Le Monde (April 1999) See: http;//www.infochangeindia.org/changemakers4.jsp

2. Ibid

Chapter 3

Plotkin,M., Medicine Quest: In Search of Nature's Hidden Cures, Viking Publishing, New York 2000.

Chapter 4

1.See note 1 in Chapter 3

2.See note 1 in Chapter 3. A remark that appeared on the web in a Reuters interview

Chapter 5

1.See web site http://www Scott London, com/insight/scripts/shiva. html

2.State of World Population 2001 See http://www.unfpa.org/swp/2001/ english/html

Chapter 6

1.Global Environment outlook 2000. Published by the United Nations Environment Programme (UNEP)

2.Do a Yahoo Search on note 1 and you will see links toPachamama: Our Earth, Our Future. The book could also be purchased via Earthprint.com

Chapter 9

1. Hawken, P., Lovins, A., & Lovins., H., Natural Capitalism: Creating the Next Industrial Revolution, Rocky Mountain Institute. See: http:/ www.rmi.org

2. Popular Science, December 2001. P.26. Or check the web site on Gorlov Helical Turbine

3. Check the web site for books written by Dr.Vandana Shiva, http:// www.mvoai.org. Also do a web search in "Vedic Agriculture."

4. Check the web site for books and interviews with Shashikala Ananth. Book excerpts available on the Website for Roli Books

5. Nader, T., The physiology of Consciousness, Maharishi University Management Press Fairfield, Iowa, USA

6. Swami Yukteswar, The Holy Science, published by The Self-Realization Fellowship, C.A

7. Ehrlich, R.R. and Ehrlich, A., Betrayal of Science and Reason: How Anti-Environmental Rhetoric Threatens our Future, A Shearwater Book published by Island Press 1996.

8. See note 1.

9. Pauli,G., "No-waste Economy", Resurgence Magazine, England (article was downloaded from http://resurgence.gn.apc.org/articles/pauli.html.)

10. See note 2.

Chapter 10

1. News-India Times, Feb 8, 2002. Published in New York.

2. See note 1 in chapter 9

3. Suzuki, D., "Ants, Antibiotics and Us" downloaded from the web site see http://www .elements.nb.ca/theme/health/david/suauki. html.

4. Search the web site by typing: Gaia Hypothesis or Gaia Theory, One would find several articles on Gaia

5. Toms, M., "The Natural Step to a Sustainable Future". New Dimensions World Broadcasting Network. See: http://www.newdimensions.org/article/robert.html.

6. Sampat., P., What does India Want", World Watch, July/Aug 1998 (article was downloaded from the web site of The world watch Institute in Washington D.C Check this web for useful publications such as The State of the World)

7. ibid.

8. Featherstone, A.W. "Planetary Healing", Resurgence Issue 211 (Downloaded the article from http://resurgence.gn.apc.org/issues/watson211.html.)

Chapter 11

1. Singhvi, Laxmi Mall H.E., "Environmental Wisdom of Ancient India", Found on http://www.ecomall.cm/greenshopping/easgree2. html.

2 . Capra, F., "Ecology and Community", This is a paper 1 downloaded from the web site Of the Centre for Ecoliteracy established by Fritjof Capra. Located in Berkeley, CA.

3. Ibid

4.Berry, T., The Dream of the Earth, Sierra Club Nature and Natural Philosophy Library, San Francisco, CA 1988 p.354-356.

5. Ibid. (See quote on cover jacket)

6.http://sustainer.org/about

References

1. Allaby, M., A guide to Gaia: A Survey of The New Science of our Living Earth, EP Dutton (a division of Penguin Books, USA) New York, N.Y 1990

2. Edmondson, B., "Where Everybody Knows Your Name". US Airways Attaché, February 2002 (An in-flight magazine published by US Airways.)

3. Ehrlich, P.R., and Ehrlich, A., Betrayal of Science and Reason: How Anti-Environmental Rhetoric Threatens our Future, A Shearwater Book published by Island Press 1996.

4. Hoyt, E., The Earth Dwellers: Adventures in the Land of Ants, Simon & Schuster, New York, N.Y.1990

5. http://www.pelothcropy.com. Also referenced websites for Zero Emissions Research Institute (ZERI) and the on line Resurgence magazine.

6. http.//www.discovering/books.com/Burbank/ I had referred to this site to know a little bit more about Luther Burbank. The interested reader is encouraged to read the works of Luther Burbank and a description of his work in The Autobiography of a Yogi written by Paramahansa Yogananda.

7. Korten, D.C When Corporations Rule the World., Kumarian Press, Inc., CT., and Berrett-Koehler Publishers, Inc., CA 1995 (The words and the concept Whole-Systems Thinking and People-Centered Power was developed from reading this book)

8. Lerner, S., Eco-Pioneers: Practical Visionaries Solving Today's Environmental Problems, MIT Press, Cambridge, MA, USA,

9. Marsh, D., "The Soul of the Soil" Resurgence Magazine. The article was downloaded from the web site: http://resurgence. gn.apc.org/issues/marsh211.htm.

10. McDonough, W., and Braungart, M., Cradle to Cradle Remaking the Way We make Things, North Point Press, May 2002.

11. Ramprasad, R., Healthcare Reborn: Innovative Essays that Will Lower costs and Improve Will Being Through Balance and Harmony, Writers Club Press an imprint of Universe, Inc. Lincoln, NE 68512., USA, 2002 ISBN: 0-595-24167-0

12. State of The World. The Worldwatch Institute publishes this book on an yearly basis. They are located in Washington, D.C., USA.

13. Zibart, R., "When the Community is the Classroom", Parade Magazine , April 28, 2002. Published in the USA.